Miracles in the Nations

A Journey across Africa and Beyond

Anne Simpson

Sunesis Ministries

Miracles in the Nations

Copyright © 2024 Anne Simpson.

The right of Anne Simpson to be identified as the author of this work has been asserted by her in accordance with the Copyright, Designs, and Patents Act 1988.

The author guarantees all contents are original and do not infringe upon the legal rights of any other person or work. All rights reserved. No part of this publication may be reproduced or transmitted in any form or by any means, electronic or mechanical, including photocopy, recording, or any information storage and retrieval system, without permission in writing from the author.

The author of this book does not dispense medical advice or prescribe the use of any technique as a form of treatment for physical, emotional, or medical problems without the advice of a physician, either directly or indirectly. The intent of the author is only to offer information of a general nature to help you in your quest for emotional and spiritual well-being. In the event you use any of the information in this book for yourself, the author and publisher assume no responsibility for your actions. The views expressed in this book are solely those of the author and do not necessarily reflect the views of the publisher, and the publisher hereby disclaims any responsibility for them.

ISBN: 978-1-9163874-9-2

Published by Sunesis Ministries
Email: info@stuartpattico.com
Website: www.stuartpattico.com

Contents

Introduction 4

1. The Call to Africa 6
2. Church in Uganda 13
3. Distributing Gifts to the Poor 17
4. Assisting Abused Children 22
5. Women's Refuge Malawi 26
6. Divine Protection 39
7. Miracles in Malawi 47
8. Miracles in Uganda 74
9. Cyclone Freddy 2023 84
10. India 87
11. Pakistan 95
12. The Adventure Continues 97
13. Going to Chitipa 103
14. Ministry in Mzuzu and Mzimba 114
15. Ministry in Lilongwe 131
16. Reflections 136

Epilogue 139

Introduction

I want to take you on a journey of discovery to the nations and share with you the amazing adventures that I have had over the years and the miracles I have seen, the lives that have been transformed and our hopes for the future.

Jesus said "Go Into all the world and make disciples of all nations "and I have been privileged to have that opportunity to go to many nations on several continents of the world and to be able to witness first-hand the power of the gospel in people's lives and how even the smallest thing can make a huge impact in people's lives. From the Children's party to 500 children in Uganda, to helping widows in Malawi set up small businesses and seeing God give people creative miracles. To witnessing the hand of God when we have been stranded in the middle of a national park at night or travelling the length of a country during a fuel crisis, we have seen the provision and protection of God. In this book I will seek to share just a few of these adventures and achievements to give you a flavour of the work that God is doing around the world and to inspire you that God can also use you to do great things too.

In every adventure, my faith has been lifted higher to believe that God can do amazing things.

This book is dedicated also to all those who have worked faithfully with me in this ministry. Those who have travelled with me and those who have stayed behind and prayed and supported. I always tell people that without those who have prayed and supported I would not be here today but together we are making a difference for the kingdom of God.

I hope that as you read this book, you will be inspired and encouraged. I believe that there is a call of God on each person's life, and I pray that God will show you the part that you can also play in helping to change lives around the world. So let me take you on a journey of discovery.

1. The Call to Africa

I had been in ministry a number of years before the call to Africa came. I had always believed in healing and miracles and throughout the first part of my ministry I had seen a few people healed but nothing much compared to what I am seeing today, and nothing compared to what I wanted to see and what I believed I should see.

I would regularly read about the miracles that Jesus and the Apostles did in the Bible where blind eyes would open and deaf ears would open and I remember crying out to God and saying, "Lord you are the same yesterday, today and forever and you said that if we lay hands on the sick they would get well, so what is the problem?" I don't remember receiving an actual answer from the Lord, but I want to encourage you to never give up on what you believe if it is scriptural. Sometimes there are delays for certain reasons. Maybe we are not yet ready to receive what he has promised us, but I want to encourage you to just keep serving God and at the right time the promises will be fulfilled.

I always believed that the sick should be healed not only by laying on hands but also just by people being brought into the presence of God. I used to read the scripture about Peter's shadow healing the sick and I used to think "what about my shadow"?

Over the years I prayed for countless people and the other thing that I came to realise is that we don't always know the results, but I believe that God allows us to know enough so that we and others can be encouraged. One time I had prayed for a lady in the north of England who was due to go to hospital the next day to have a tumour removed. It wasn't until I returned to that same meeting a year later that the lady came to tell me that after I had prayed for her, she returned to the hospital the next day for the operation, and they did a pre check before the operation and were amazed to find that there was no tumour! If I had not returned to that same meeting a year later, I would never have known about this miracle, so I want to encourage you to keep praying whether you know the results or not. The results are up to God – our part is to pray and release healing by faith. Another time I had prayed for a lady who was pregnant, and they told her that the babies she was carrying would be deformed. I prayed for her that night and did not hear the results for nearly 10 years when I finally bumped into the lady who told me that after prayer the twins were born healthy and now living a normal life. I believe that when we get to heaven, we will be amazed at the impact of our prayers in people's lives.

So, as you can see, I was seeing miracles, but these were just a few compared to the amount of people I was praying for, but God was preparing me for the future.

Coming from the UK I often hear people saying that miracles only happen in places like Africa, but I want to encourage you that miracles happen wherever people are open to receive by faith. God does not change when I get on an airplane, I do not change when I exit the plane on the soil of Africa, but it is the people's faith and expectation levels that draw out the anointing and can create an atmosphere for miracles.

One such evening before going to Africa happened again in the north of England. I had been invited to speak at a ladies meeting and had intended to speak about miracles, but God had another idea and instead wanted to demonstrate miracles.

As I got up to speak, suddenly the presence of God fell in the room, and I was not able to speak. Instead, I began to look around and saw the Holy Spirit touching people and suddenly a lady at the back cried out that she had been healed and threw away her crutches and came running to the front, then one by one people began coming forward saying that pain had left their bodies – hallelujah.

I left that meeting so encouraged not just because of the miracles but because it was what I had always believed should happen. No one had laid hands on anyone; they had simply come into the presence of God and on top of all that I left the meeting saying "This happened in the UK not In Africa "!

Therefore, when I now tell people about the miracles that I see In Africa and people say, "I wish we could see them here". I am able to share my experiences that yes, they also happen here, in fact they will happen anywhere that people are open to receive.

When I began to see regular miracles, people asked me "What did you suddenly do differently?" And I told them that I didn't do anything differently, but I just kept going and didn't give up and eventually God gave me a breakthrough. I believe that this is true in many areas of our lives – if you believe something then keep going and don't give up because eventually you will gain the victory.

Now let me add here that I don't see every person healed and in fact I lost a very close friend to a brain tumour during the time of COVID even though I had prayed and believed for her to be healed. At the time I could not understand but God gave me a peace to carry on and it has in no way changed my views on healing even though we may not understand all things. I hear many different views on healing but most of them are based on our experience, not the word of God. If we will keep doing what Jesus told us to do, then he will bring the results.

Around 2010 I began to get a sense that God was calling me to Africa although I have to admit that I did not want to go and in fact had always said that I would never go to Africa!

One day I was praying because I was frustrated about the lack of response to the gospel in this country and as I was praying, I saw myself throwing bread on the water and suddenly all these ducks appeared hurrying to eat the bread that I had thrown like they were so hungry. Then I remember reflecting on what I was praying, and I suddenly realised that I had also been asking God about Africa and I remember thinking "oh no!"

I often look back and think that God's plans are often not our plans and that also he doesn't show us everything at once or else we would not even begin. I also remember that there was a man in a house group that I attended who had a picture as he was praying for me, and he saw me preaching and surrounded by thousands of black people and again I told him that I am not going to Africa! And I remember him saying to me "I can't help what I have seen".
So, for a while Africa had been coming up on my radar but I had been ignoring it.

Then one day I went to visit a lady who moves in the prophetic and as she prayed for me, she gave me a word that God was going to use me to do creative miracles, but I would need to go to Africa to pick up the anointing. I remember thinking "can I have the creative miracle anointing without going to Africa "
However, I decided to just pray over the word thinking that it might be for the distant future. Then just a few weeks later I

had an email from another lady minister inviting me to join the team that she was taking out to Uganda that summer! I remember sitting looking at my computer thinking "oh my goodness, this is God – now what am I going to do?"

I remember praying about it for a while and decided that because I wanted this creative miracle anointing that I would go, but I decided that I would only go for a short time and that I would only go once! Considering that 13 years later I have been countless times and even spent 8 months there during the covid lockdown, I am sure that God was having a good laugh to himself but in his wisdom, he did not show me anything further ahead than that one mission otherwise he knew that I would never have got on the plane that first time.

I have to say that God very quickly changed my heart and that after that first trip, I slowly changed my mind and now I love going to Africa and consider it to be my second home and have connected to so many amazing people over the years but in the beginning, it was an act of obedience to do something that I didn't really want to do.

Upon arrival in Uganda, I ministered in several churches and made a connection with the Blessed Highway Christian Church near Kampala that has been an ongoing relationship until today and I will share more of that in another chapter. I also met my spiritual daughter who was only 3 years old at the time who I have supported all these years and had the privilege of seeing her having her 16th birthday party recently which was amazing. My first time preaching in the Blessed Highway was when the church had poles and sheets, and it flooded the first night I preached, and all the electricity went out leaving me standing in the dark and a flood. Today that same church is now a concrete-built building with a stage and lighting and an office and inside toilet and recently we even bought the land next door for children's church, bible school and administration offices. I have witnessed transformations of not only lives but infrastructure as well during the years that I have been visiting and ministering in Africa.

During this first visit we visited prayer mountain and all the time I was wondering where I would "pick up this anointing I had been promised"?

Then one night I went to another church and as we were in worship, I suddenly saw the hand of God throw something at me and he said "there you are ". I was left feeling a little underwhelmed because it didn't seem very dramatic. I have since come to realise that most things God does are not dramatic although the outcome might be dramatic. Like when Elijah was looking for the presence of God on the mountain, there was thunder and lightning, but the Lord was not in them, instead he was in the gentle whisper. Sometimes we miss the gentle whisper because we are looking for the dramatic.
So here I am in the meeting wondering "was that it?". Then the pastor gets up and looks at me and says "because you came, God has put a new anointing on your life ". Wow! That was my confirmation, and the key was "because you came ". Because I did something by faith that I didn't really want to do then God blessed me. The key was obedience.

Many times in the bible we see that God asked people to do things that didn't make sense at the time, but as they obeyed, then results came – like when God instructed Joshua to march around the walls of Jericho 7 times blowing trumpets and shouting so that the walls would come down. It didn't make sense to their natural minds but because they obeyed the walls came down and they entered into their promise. For me, I didn't know what would happen when I first boarded that flight to Uganda, but I realise now that I would have missed half of my destiny if I had not obeyed and went even when I was apprehensive to go.

I remember when I got on the plane to come home, I still didn't think I would be returning. As the plane took off, I said, "ok God I did it". God was probably laughing again.

As I returned home to the UK and reflected on the trip, the Lord began to lay the Blessed Highway church on my heart, and I began to communicate with the Pastor who then invited me to return to conduct a women's conference the following Easter and there the story really begins...

From that second trip to speak at the Easter Conference I began to make connections that would then take me not only around Uganda but into Kenya and Rwanda and from there into Malawi and Tanzania

It all began with one willingness to say "yes", and the rest is history, and the story is still being written.

2. Church in Uganda

From my first visit and the connection with the Blessed Highway church I began to work with the pastor there and even travelling to Kenya and Rwanda through our connections.

When I first arrived, as I mentioned earlier the church was looking very bad and was also only on rented land. I began to prophesy that God was going to send a businessman to help them to buy the land. I am not sure what happened to the businessman but our ministry over a number of years assisted them to first buy the land and then to build a permanent structure building. When I look at the before and after photos, it is amazing what God has done and every step has been a step of faith and has not been without struggles. I have come to realise that land in Africa is territorial and spiritual, and in the beginning, there was a lot of opposition to the church buying the land but through prayer the battle was won, and victory came. Now there is not only a good-looking church structure but also an office and an inside toilet for visiting speakers which has been a real blessing. I remember in the past when it was raining heavily, and I needed to use the bathroom before speaking and had to go running outside in the rain and came back soaking wet before getting up on the platform to speak so having the inside bathroom has been a big blessing.

As I mentioned earlier, my very first night preaching at this church was when it was just a temporary structure of tarpaulin and wooden poles and no floor, just dust. Halfway through preaching heavy rains came and all the electricity went out! I was standing in the dark with a flood coming around my feet and trying to carry on preaching as normal while people tried to make some light from their phones. This was my first experience of preaching in Africa, but I have since learnt that these things are quite normal during rainy season especially in rural areas or where the church does not have a permanent structure.

There are so many things that we take for granted in the west, like inside bathrooms, inside kitchens with running water, electricity that works all the time but in a lot of places in Africa these things are seen as a luxury.

When I first visited this church, the land next to the church was also for sale and I remember prophesying that the church would also own that land. One Sunday I asked the church to prepare communion and during the service I went outside with the communion wine and anointed the land next door and claimed it for the church. It took a number of years and several setbacks and battles but eventually the land was bought, and they now plan to build a building that will be multi-purpose including a bible school, children's church and church offices along with a car parking area. We have certainly come a long way since that first visit but am believing that we are going to go even further with the help of God. The church is now a shining light in the area and reaching many people with the love of God.

Children's Christmas Party

One year I was privileged to be in Uganda over Christmas, and we decided to hold a party for the children. My church at the time decided to buy presents of books and pens, teddy bears and other toys and carefully wrap them all for me to take out. I arrived at London Heathrow with a trolley full of oversized bags and went to the check in where I was told that my bags were too big for the conveyer belt, and I would have to go to the oversize department. However, the lady at check in put labels on my bags which I later saw were over 34 kg each and directed me to the oversize department. Upon arriving at the oversize department, a man took each bag and sent them off on his conveyer belt and all without any extra charge which must have been the favour of God because other times I have been asked to take items out of my bags when I am only a few kg over the limit.

Upon arrival in Uganda, we got ready for the children's party which the pastor had told me there would be 200 children attending, but upon arriving at the church we found that the place was full and around 500 children had gathered. They were given food and drinks and entertainment and then I was asked to give a word and nearly every child received Jesus – hallelujah.

We then began to give out the presents hoping that they would multiply and stretch so that every child could receive something. I will never forget the look on some of their faces as they received their gifts. One young girl had received a teddy bear - maybe the first in her life and she was holding it and looking at it with sheer delight in her face. Others were stampeding just to receive a pencil once they could see that the presents were not enough for everyone. Compared to here in the U.K, where those things would mean nothing, these simple gifts were able to bring joy to the children's hearts. I remember one time In Malawi where we had given out items of second-hand clothes and one young boy came up to me to say "thank you for my new shoes "and they were only a basic make second hand and yet his heart was full of joy.

That day as we left the church, we saw children walking up the road smiling and singing as they took their gifts with them but most of all that day, they took the greatest gift home and that was Jesus.

3. Distributing Gifts to the Poor

Nearly every time that I go to Africa, I always take at least one or maybe two extra bags with me to bless people in the various churches and villages that I visit. Again, in the west we are blessed to have so many things and I always say to people that getting things is not a problem but transporting them is the problem. I have had several situations where I have sent things by cargo ship and found that only some of the things arrive at their correct destination so it is a joy when we can carry things ourselves and have the privilege of actually seeing the people receive their gifts. In the U.K I enjoy going to charity shops and car boot sales and the amount of second hand or even new clothes that you see is amazing. We have given out clothes in the villages, essential toiletries and even toys for the children who may have never received a teddy bear before in their life. In fact, I have been in people's homes where if they have a teddy bear, it is displayed in a cabinet as something of great value not just played with. One time in Malawi we went with a bag of knitted teddies that someone had made and given to us to take. The pastor called for the children in the area to come and there was such a rush of children that there was not enough for everyone and even weeks later children were still arriving at the pastors' house asking for teddy bears!

To see the smile on people's faces from receiving the smallest gifts is amazing.

One time a team went into another remote village in Malawi and gave out small cloths that they call "Chitenje "to the women that they found at the well. The pastor told me that the women were crying with gratitude at receiving this simple gift.

Other times we have given gifts of mattresses as many of the homes in the villages don't have complete beds, but the people just sleep with a mat on the floor.

Being welcomed into people's homes is an honour and even though they don't have much, they are willing to share what they have. It is customary when visiting someone in Africa to take a gift of some kind and it is also customary that if a visitor arrives, they should be given something to eat.

One time I had been invited to different homes in Malawi to pray for people. We began at the first house and as we entered, we were asked to sit down, and we found that they had prepared a table of breakfast for us which was very nice, and we ate and enjoyed and then prayed for the family but not realising that we would have to do this at 3 houses in one morning! By the time I got to the third house, I had to very kindly try to say they I could only eat a banana!

So, although we take gifts, they also give what they are able to us as well especially in the area of hospitality and eating. A lot of the areas we visit are farming areas so although they may be materially poor, they can offer food and many times we have also found that after doing a conference they will also want to bring us an offering as a sign of their gratitude and it is often in terms of food items, produce from their land. I have received bunches of bananas, cassava, potatoes, pineapple and the big one is chickens. A lot of people in the villages only eat meat on special occasions but when a visitor arrives, they will prepare a chicken and also give a live chicken as a gift which is a high honour. I remember one time in Uganda when we had completed a 3-day conference and on the day, we were leaving, different people wanted to bring us their appreciation and we ended up going back to Kampala with 6 live chickens tied to the roof rack of the car! A very usual sight in Africa!

Several times when I have been in Malawi, we have organised a special time during a conference to buy gifts of essential items like rice, sugar, salt, soap and to call the poorest people from the area to come – often the elderly and widowed or single mothers and they are invited to attend the Sunday service and then at the end they also receive their gifts. We have found that by doing this, they also have an opportunity to hear the gospel and receive the greatest gift of salvation in Jesus Christ.

Many times, the Pastors' will go out to the remote villages to preach and will also take with them gifts of food and other essential items. Jesus himself gave us the example when he preached to the 5,000. As well as preaching to them, he also fed them. Jesus taught us that we should not just preach with words but with action as well. It is hard for someone to listen to a message of hope if they are hungry and have nothing to eat or nowhere to sleep so we try to combine preaching with also assisting their practical needs as well although it is not possible to help every person due to the huge needs in Africa but I remember some time back when I was pondering that and the Lord said " you can't help everyone but you can help the one In front of you " and also we are not called to help everyone personally but if God has given us a position of influence then we can use that influence to tell stories like I am doing now and allow God to touch the hearts of others to also assist. I have found that when I come back from a mission trip, I will often not only give reports of the salvations and healing that have taken place, but I will also tell personal stories of people's lives that I have encountered along the way and through this I have found that God has prompted people's hearts to support and together we begin to make a difference.

One such story that I must mention here is 2 boys – Joshua and Isaac who were orphaned in Uganda when their father killed their mother and then killed himself leaving 2 young boys in a very traumatic state. The boys went to live with their uncle in the village but were not happy and wanted to go to live with the Pastor and his wife in Kampala and although they were willing to take them, they were not able to afford it and their house was also not big enough. However, by telling their story back home, we were able to assist the pastor to move to a bigger home and those boys are now thriving under the care of the Pastor and his wife. To see the before and after photos of these boys is amazing. I remember when I first visited them after losing their parents and they were very traumatised and sad and withdrawn and now they are 2 happy smiling boys on their way to a very bright future.

Another time at a meeting in Malawi the Lord directed me to give a lady a small amount of money and told her that God was anointing her to start a small business. I then had the privilege of returning to that same place a year later and the same lady told me that after receiving that money she went to buy 5 chickens – 2 of the chickens died but the others survived and also multiplied and now she had many chickens which were producing eggs for her which not only fed her family but she was also selling the eggs for an income and as a token of her appreciation she came to the meeting and presented me with one chicken as her offering back to me.

Stories like this make everything worthwhile when you see that what you are doing is making a difference in people's lives.

Another time I had a prophetic word for a lady which turned out to be true because her husband had died, and she was left to bring up several children by herself and she had nothing. After talking with her I asked her what kind of things she was gifted at and what she would like to do. She told me that she wanted to run a small kiosk selling teas and bakery. We managed to assist her with a small capital to find a place to rent and some essential ingredients to begin. As I handed her the money, she fell down on the floor crying and thanking God. Another example of how small things mean a lot. That lady then went and started her small business and was able to provide for her family.

Another time in Uganda we bought pigs that were distributed to different people in the community so that they could make a living for themselves.

At the women's refuge in Malawi every lady was given a small capital to begin a business, but I will share more about that in a later chapter.

There is saying "give a man a fish and he will eat for a day but teach him how to fish and he will eat every day".

So, although we go and we do help and we do distribute goods, we also try to empower people to begin helping themselves and rising out of their place of poverty.

4. Assisting Abused Children

One very disturbing thing that we have come to see while working in Africa is the number of children not only living in poverty but also how so many suffer abuse that often goes unnoticed by the outside world.

A few years back I began to read about stories of children in Malawi who were being burnt by either their parents or neighbours or other relatives as a form of punishment. I began to pray over this situation which to me and many others here seemed shocking, and I began to ask the Lord how we could help in this situation and also, I asked the Lord to help me to bring awareness of what was taking place. Maybe even this book will bring some awareness as well.

I want to share one such story which has turned out to be a miracle story of a transformed life and how God takes a hold of a negative situation and turns it around for his glory. I have called it – Saudi - a story of grace.

A few years back I was told about a young boy who was living in a very remote village and was living with his mother who was blind, and they were in extreme poverty and the boy was often left feeling hungry due to the circumstances. One day due to him feeling hungry he went to the neighbour's house and saw some food and because he was starving, he took some of it to eat. Unfortunately, the neighbours caught him and as a punishment they took his hands and burnt them over the charcoal stove used for cooking outside. The boy's hands were severely burnt, and he was left in a traumatic state. I came to learn about this situation and decided that we had to do something to help although at the time I had no idea how much God would do in this situation.

So, I began by telling people about this boy and what had happened, and we managed to pay for his medical costs so he could go to a proper hospital and get treatment for his burns. I then wanted to know more about his family life and who was taking care of him and if the mother was a good person.

This involved the Pastor going into a very remote village where we had to hire a 4/4 vehicle and even then, the Pastor had to walk the last few miles due to the nature of the roads being impassable and the journey was also during rainy season which is like monsoon conditions in Malawi. Upon arrival at the boy's village, we found that it was very poor and very remote, but his mother Beatrice was a good mother, but she was blind, and her husband had left her a long time ago and he had also been abusive, so she was left struggling to take care of her children. I also wanted to know why Beatrice was blind and was she born like that or did something happen to her. The Pastor told me that she had been born with one blind eye but then her husband beat her, and she went completely blind. We then decided to try to support Beatrice and also to look for a school for Saudi as well.

The testimony of this story is that Saudi has now been at boarding school for the past 3 years and is now thriving and doing really well in his education and who knows what his future will be. Maybe the update will be in another book but what I see is that God took a terrible situation and turned it around for his glory. There are many millions of suffering children in Africa who will continue to grow up in poverty and yet God chose this boy out of many to have a new opportunity. If he had not been burnt, we would never have heard about him so although it was horrendous what happened, it actually became the key to his destiny. God saw him and picked him out for a future beyond what he was expecting.

When Saudi first went to boarding school, he had never been out of the village and had never received much education so arriving at a boarding school in town and especially after the traumatic experience was difficult for him and he struggled in the first year but he persevered with the encouragement of the pastor and now I see him smiling as a young teenager and his teachers are now pleased with his progress.

We also continue to help Beatrice and we are also believing that God can also restore her sight as well.

Another amazing testimony of this story is that through going to this village and the help that we gave; the chief of the village became aware of what we had done to help this family and so he invited us to go and plant a church in his village. A team went out to conduct a 3-day mission where 150 people came to the Lord and from that mission a church was established in the village, and we appointed a pastor and bought him a motorbike so he could be travelling to visit the people in the village.

So, from one horrendous act of abuse, God brought support for a family, education for a boy and a church in the village. This is the God who turns all things around for good – hallelujah.

But as I pondered on all this, my heart is that Saudi is just one of thousands like him and may God open a door for us to be able to help many others. Our dream is that in the future we may even be able to have a home for those who don't have any one to take care of them and to be able to give them a good education and opportunities in life.

The situation in Malawi at the time of writing is very difficult, the value of the Kwacha has gone down, and the prices of things have gone up and they are also in the middle of another fuel crisis, but God is faithful, and I believe that one by one lives are being transformed.

I remember hearing this little story which sums up a lot of our ministry.

There was a boy on the beach picking up star fish and throwing them back into the sea and his father said to him "I don't know why you bother because there are so many that you can never make a difference ". The boy thought about the statement for a while and then he picked up another star fish and looked at it and said "but it made a difference to this one "

That is our ministry – we may look and think that there are thousands of needs, and we can never make a difference, or we can look at the one and say, "but it made a difference to this one"!

For every Saudi, for every Beatrice, for every Joshua and Isaac we can make a difference and if all of us made a difference to one then the world would be a better place and I also believe that as we help the one with the small that we have then God multiplies and helps us to do more.

5. Women's Refuge Malawi

Over the time that I have been visiting Malawi, one of the things that seemed to touch my heart was the plight of the women who were abused or widowed or abandoned and had nowhere to go and no way of supporting themselves. There is no social security and hardly any places of refuge in Malawi, so for those who are not educated and have no way of supporting themselves, it leaves many in vulnerable situations where they may put up with abusive behaviour from bad relationships because they have no other way of taking care of themselves without a man. Often women will resort to prostitution as a way of taking care of themselves and their children which obviously is degrading and also carries a lot of risks including being beaten or killed or contracting sexually transmitted diseases as well as HIV which is very prevalent in Africa.

So, we began to think about how we could assist these women to not only have a safe place to stay but also to empower them to be able to start small businesses so that they could take care of themselves and their children without needing to be in vulnerable situations.

A few years back I was ministering in the north of Malawi in a town called Chitipa – right at the very top of Malawi bordering to Tanzania. I often call Chitipa the home of miracles as I see so many amazing things happen there, some of which I will share later. In the past Chitipa was a very hard place to get to and required several days journey from the capital of Lilongwe due to the impassable roads through the mountains and it was like a forgotten place but due to the faithful prayers of the Pastor and people at Heaven Embassy along with many other faithful pastors in the area it has transformed into a place where God is moving powerfully and a church that was only around 50 people when I first visited, is now standing room only on a Sunday and they are building an extension outside. Considering the journey from Lilongwe still takes 2 days with a stopover in Mzuzu on the way – I often say that I would not travel there if it wasn't for the amazing things that I see there. Although the roads have improved from years ago, they are still very mountainous and full of potholes but some of the scenery along the way is breathtaking as you wind around mountain passes where you can feed the wild monkeys' bananas out of the window and as you emerge and see the stunning lake down below. I have always said that Malawi has many hidden treasures and could make much more out of tourism if they invested in better infrastructure and facilities as I was surprised the first time that I went as to how much natural beauty Malawi has and the majority of the people are warm and hospitable. Indeed, Malawi is known as the warm heart of Africa.

So, it was one time when I was in Chitipa that the Lord said to me "I want you to buy land". At the time I wasn't sure exactly what for, but I shared with the Pastor who then took me to see several pieces of land that were for sale in the area. One of the pieces of land that we now own stood out to me. It was a large piece of land overlooking the mountains and with many palm trees on it and it seemed to have a peaceful feel about it. I knew then that this was the piece of land that God wanted me to buy for the work of God.

Buying land In Africa is different to buying land in the west and I would later learn that there is public land which is available for sale and then there is customary land which belongs to the chief. I did not realise at the time that we were buying customary land and so a series of years and negotiations later we came to the place of the chief signing the land completely over into our hands.

After purchasing the land, the task of building began. Everything has been by faith and when we first purchased the land, we didn't know how we would begin to build anything as we had no money for building but by faith, we had bought the land. Slowly, slowly we managed to begin building step by step over the years. The first task was to take a lot of the palm trees out of the land which would hinder us from building, and this was done by hand by the people from the church. I never cease to be amazed at the strength of the African people who do not have all the big machinery that we use for building but do everything by hand especially in the villages, so I watched as they managed to dig up and remove 50 palm trees just by using very basic equipment.

Our next task was to dig a foundation around the land, and we then went and prayed around the whole land and pouring communion wine on the land to cleanse it from any curses that had been upon the land and to set it apart and dedicate it for kingdom purposes.

Over the years we slowly began to construct a 4-room house which initially was going to be a 4-bedroom house with shared living room but actually ended up as 4 self-contained rooms with kitchen and a shared outside bathroom and toilet.

While the house was being built, we had the opportunity of renting a house where 10 young ladies moved in to and were assisted into a safe place to stay while we continued on building our own building. On one visit we went into the local market to buy furnishing for the house and were able to purchase mattresses and rugs for the floor and curtains and kitchen utensils. It always saddens me because I wanted to be able to put proper furniture and, in the UK, we have so many second-hand shops selling decent furniture for very cheap prices that here I could have furnished the whole house for a very cheap price but In Malawi second hand things do not exist or if they do, you would not want them! In the west we live in a throw away society, so someone may replace their sofa just because they want a change of colour but In Africa people will use something until it is worn out. So, I was wanting to make the house look nice but especially in chitipa you can only buy new things which are expensive. I did one time buy a sofa from the U.K and put in with a container with other things but unfortunately it was not able to be transported the other end.

I remember as I was looking around the market at the rugs and curtains and the Pastor was laughing at me because I wanted the colours to match! He couldn't see the significance of why colours must match – I guess it must be an English lady thing!

I also remember giving the ladies a kettle as they had electricity in the house that we rented (a rare commodity) and everyone was laughing and wondering how long the kettle would last as most of them had probably never used a kettle before as most African women from the villages are used to walking to the well to get water and boiling it on a charcoal stove outside. So, a kettle was probably a very strange concept to them. I remember also showing them how to do the washing up with the washing up liquid and a sponge with hot water while they looked at me wondering what I was doing. You will also find most African women doing their laundry outside with a bowl of water and a bar of soap. A washing machine would only be found in rich people's homes or in hotels and so every day you see the women bent over their bowl of water doing the family laundry and hanging it over anything that they can find to dry.

To this day a 4 room building stands on our land, and we have housed many different ladies over the years and sometimes even with their children. We recently appointed 2 lady pastors who have been going to visit the ladies to encourage them with bible study and prayer and to talk over issues that they have in their lives. Every time I go, I make sure to have time to speak with the ladies and to see the progress that they are having and the hopes that they have for their future.

Most of the initial group of ladies went on to be successful in the next chapter of their lives either through starting small businesses or some went back to education and some remarried. As each group left, then they were replaced with the next group of women who were needing help.

We have also distributed a small amount of money to each lady so that they can start small businesses to be able to support themselves and their children. Some have decided to sell fish or tomatoes or make doughnuts to sell at the market and some even sell second hand clothes and there is a small church shop that sells second hand clothes and some of the women work there as well. The bundles of clothes are transported from Lilongwe and interestingly most of the bundles come from the U.K as they say our clothes are the best quality. It is quite funny to go to Chitipa and see clothes from Marks and Spencer's!

Tailoring workshops

We also assisted the women by sending out sewing machines on a container so that they could begin to learn tailoring and a good teacher was found and the women went through a training on how to sew and mend clothes which a lot of women do in Africa. Whenever you go to the market you will find lots of African material for sale and a lot of women make their own clothes rather than buying them ready made. In fact, often one of the gifts that I will be given after a conference along with the chickens and bananas is a piece of African cloth that can be made into a dress at the local tailors. I have often come back with a wide assortment of African fabrics. So, people here donated some sewing machines, and they were sent out so that the women were able to use this skill to earn a living.

Wedding dress hire

We also sent out some wedding dresses which they used to hire out to people when they were having a wedding. Up to now this has not worked as well as we were hoping but I believe that it still has great potential and maybe it is just a case of wrong place, wrong time.

In every place it is trying to identify what works best for the area that we are working in.

All of the women have become dedicated members of the church and some of the women are even part of the intercessory group who pray all night in the church when special events are coming up. One time when I was in Uganda, the Pastor told me that the ladies are in the church praying and fasting every night until you come to visit us here too. Needless to say, it was inevitable that I had to leave from Uganda and go to Chitipa! The welcome that I receive in Chitipa is like royalty has arrived and I guess in one sense it has because the bible says that we are a royal priesthood, and we are ambassadors for Christ.

One time I had been travelling 6 hours from Mzuzu to Chitipa and was expecting to just go to my guest house and rest when I arrived and use the bathroom and have a very English cup of tea, but as we were nearing to Chitipa the Pastor suddenly tells me that everyone is waiting in the church service for me! My natural side wanted to say "let me rest and I go to the church tomorrow "but I knew how much my visit meant to these people. So, I decided to just stop at the guest house for half an hour to refresh myself and then go to the church where obviously I was also expected to preach and pray for people. One thing that I have learnt over the years is that when you are tired, the Holy Spirit is never tired. As I entered the church, I receive such a standing ovation that it was hard to be tired anymore. I can't remember what I preached that day, but I do know that I went back to my guest house that evening feeling very happy that I had made the effort to go straight to the church. Another time there was an overnight service and they wanted me to preach at midnight and at the time I was just feeling like going to bed but as I went to preach so many amazing miracles took place that it was worth every sacrifice.

I believe that this honour that I receive is the key to why so many miracles happen here – some of which I will share in another chapter.

New bathroom and toilet block

On one visit in 2021 I arrived to find that the original toilet block was sinking in the ground and was no longer safe for the women to use and so began the next few weeks of raising money for a new toilet block to be built. Again, as I mentioned earlier about the people who lifted 50 palm trees out with their hands – now also a pit latrine was dug out by 2 young men with pix axes in the scorching heat – so amazing.

Most of the public toilets in Africa especially in the villages are not like we know in the west but are often just a hole in the ground. I have had many interesting experiences of using the African toilets and during the day I just about manage but would struggle if it was during the night but most of the time, I have been blessed to be able to travel back to a decent guest house when we have been out in the villages. I remember one village where the outside toilet was built of bamboo and was so narrow that I had to duck down and walk sideways to get in and was then wondering how I would get out again! Factor in the fact that you often also have things crawling around and flies buzzing around, I always pray that I don't need to spend too long. Even after all these years I have still not quite mastered the art of squatting and aiming properly!!

And so here we have these 2 young men digging the pit latrine before we can then begin to build the surrounds and doors etc.

As often happens in Africa – I began with a budget of £400 which ended up over £1,000 by the time we had finished due to the rising costs of everything.

Along with the pit latrines, we also built a bathroom – now when I say a bathroom I am not talking about showers and wash basins. I remember one lady asking me if we were now going to put in the fixtures and fittings – to which I replied "there are no fixtures and fittings apart from the door "!

Most bathrooms In Africa especially in the villages are just a room where you put your bucket of water and wash by pouring a jug over yourself and that is often after the women have walked to collect the water in the first place and carried it back in buckets on their heads and then warmed it up over the charcoal stove if they want a warm bath.

Obviously in towns it is different, and I have stayed in people's homes in town that are of the same standard that we would find in the west, so these conditions are not everywhere but are more common in the villages. I remember the very first time that I went to Africa wondering about where I would sleep and what I would eat because often our only understanding of Africa if we haven't been is what we see on the TV with mud huts and dusty roads and believe me these do exist but I have also stayed in places nicer than here so until you go, you only have a limited understanding of Africa. Africa is a diverse mix of cultures and traditions and different standards according to where you are and also when we generalise Africa, we are not talking of a country but a continent and the continent of Africa is comprised of 54 countries so there is so much diversity.

So, after a couple of weeks, I was able to see the new toilets and bathroom finished before leaving to go to the next place. We also decided to do a light-hearted competition to name the new toilet block and the winner of the prize went to the man who named it "LuLu".

It was also during this time that we began the process of bringing in the ministry of lands to give us the drawings of the land so that we could begin the application for the title deeds of the land which was another long process like most things in Africa.

So, to date there are 10 women staying in the house, some were abandoned by their husbands, some were widowed and had nothing to be able to sustain themselves. According to some local cultural practices, some women after losing their husband also lose their house as the family of the husband come to claim it for themselves forcing the lady to leave. Many of these women are not properly educated and don't understand that if they had applied to the courts, they would probably have been legally entitled to keep the house, but many don't understand their rights and the culture in the villages can be so strong that they just accept what they are told.

As mentioned earlier the economy of Malawi is very bad at this time and the prices of things have gone very high so even with their small businesses, many are finding it hard to afford to be able to buy food and so we also send a small amount each month to help with their daily needs. The church has also purchased some land for farming and the women are being taught how to farm so that they can use some for their own food and some to sell as an income as well.

In the villages, farming is one of their biggest ways of surviving so they are very dependent upon the weather and if it is too dry or too wet, they can lose a whole harvest resulting in a whole year of near starvation for many families. Malawi has suffered several devastating cyclones recently that have knocked out a whole year's supply of crops as well as many people losing their homes and their lives and this year of 2023 was a particularly bad cyclone where many lost their lives, and I will share more about that in another chapter.

Another area that the people have struggled recently is with the cost of fertiliser rising sharply and so we have been trying to encourage them towards sustainable farming without the need of buying fertiliser. This will help them to be able to grow crops to feed their families and also to have some produce to be able to sell for an income as well. They have recently begun training on how to make their own compost so that it can save them buying fertiliser and it is better for their crops as well, and we recently received photos of them putting into practice the new farming techniques that they have been learning. This will greatly assist them to be able to sustain themselves and their families by not only providing crops to eat but the remainder can be sold as an income for the family.

Future plans

The land that we purchased is large and after the initial piece of land that we purchased, we were then offered 2 additional pieces of land bordering our land for ridiculous prices which seemed silly to turn down even though we didn't know what we were going to do with them at the time but I concluded that God must have a purpose if he was giving it to us so I decided to buy the extra 2 plots of land. I also heard that the people selling the additional pieces of land were people who had benefited from my ministry at the church and so they wanted to give the land to me almost as an offering but obviously had to charge just a nominal amount. One of the pieces of land borders to where we could make a road in the future for better ease of access as at the moment we have to park and walk to get to where the house is although this isn't a big problem at the moment but in the future, we are believing to have our own entrance from the road.

So, with all this extra land we have plans first for a mission house where myself and other team members can stay when we are there rather than needing to stay in the guest house spending money. It could also double up as a guest house for paying guests when we are not there, which would also raise money for the ministry. We would also like to set up a training centre where the community can be trained in various skills for life and even to be able to expand the amount of accommodation that we could offer to other women in need. We are believing that God gave us this extra land for a purpose and in his time, he will supply the finances needed to be able to expand the work. Another thing that is needed is a concrete wall around all of our land to give the privacy and protection needed. We believe that what God has begun he will complete.

As I travel around Malawi, I see the increasing need for more help for these women and for further education on things like gender-based violence and I am happy to say that there are now many NGO's who are addressing these issues and slowly attitudes towards women are changing but there are still many challenges but through education things are beginning to improve. A lot of girls in villages do not go to school due to poverty of families not being able to afford school fees and, in a family, where there are several children, they will give priority to the boys going to school. This means that many girls grow up without a proper education which then leads to them being vulnerable to abuse in their adult life. If a woman is not able to earn her own money and is totally dependent upon the man, then it can lead to problems if she wishes to leave the marriage due to abuse but has no way of supporting herself so many women remain in situations that are not good because they have no other way of surviving.

One such story stands out on this issue. I was preaching in a village not far from Chitipa and I had a word of knowledge about someone with an ear problem. A young lady came to the front to say that since her husband had beaten her, she had not been able to hear properly. My heart went out to this young lady but then the response of the congregation as they laughed at this lady's story made a righteous anger rise up inside of me at why the congregation thought this was funny. So, after praying for the lady who was instantly healed of all pain and could also hear properly again, I then became to speak to the Pastor and the congregation telling them that God does not think these things are funny and I encouraged the pastor to speak out to change attitudes where many think that these things are normal. My prayer is that attitudes will begin to change.

Afterwards I had an opportunity to talk with the lady privately because I wanted to know if she was now in a safe situation, and I found out that she had divorced the husband and was now living alone with her children. I managed to just give her a small amount of money to help with some food and asked the pastor to keep an eye on her. The sad thing is that this lady is just one of many going through difficult situations and unlike in the west it is hard for women to leave their abusive situations unless they are educated and working because there is no help from the government, no housing benefit so if the woman cannot earn her own money then she is at the mercy of the abuser and will often stay in the situation because she has nowhere else to go. This is why we are trying to not only provide a safe house but to empower women to stand.

6. Divine Protection

Psalm 91 v 9-11 "If you make the Most High your dwelling, then no harm will befall you, no disaster will come near your tent for he will command his angels concerning you to guard you in all your ways".

Sometimes people ask me if going to Africa is dangerous and the answer is Yes and No. Of course, there are places that are dangerous but then that is the same in lots of places in the world. I believe that the safest place to be is in the centre of God's will because then there is protection from God. We also use wisdom in not wandering around by ourselves and being with local people although the story that I am about to share probably did not involve much wisdom.

I want to share a few stories that have happened during my travels to highlight the protection of God. I am sure that there are many more times that I was protected without even knowing. I am so blessed to have people who pray for me while I am on mission, and I know that without them things would not work the way that they do. There is a story in the Bible where the Israelites were fighting against the Amalekites and Moses went up to the top of the mountain and held up the staff of God while Joshua and the army were fighting in the valley. While Moses hands were up, the Israelites were winning but when his hands grew tired and they began to lower, then they began losing the battle. I believe that this represents prayer and those that stand with us on the mountain while we are in the valley. Nothing happens without prayer, and I am so grateful to those who stand with me in prayer as well as financial support.

Nyika National Park

The first story that I want to share is one time when I was in the north of Malawi and on our day off the Pastor offered to take me and another lady that I was travelling with to the national park to see the wild animals. We were both excited at the prospect of seeing the animals and so we set off for our day out or so we thought!

As we travelled along it soon became evident that the roads were very bad and were not suitable for the kind of car that we were in. However, we foolishly decided to try to continue anyway! After several attempts at revving the car uphill with wheels spinning and the car constantly overheating and several attempts at asking local people how much further it was to the national park and being told "not far, just round the corner, just over this hill"! I have since come to realise that asking locals for directions does not often lead to a correct answer and many just around the corners later, we found ourselves to be completely stuck with the car over heating and refusing to go anywhere. So now we were in the middle of the mountains and wondering what we were going to do next. Several Pastors kept calling to offer sympathy and prayer, but no one was offering to do anything practical to help us. We then decided to try to call the park ranger to see if they could come and rescue us but by this time it was beginning to get dusk as it always gets dark quite early in Africa so the park ranger told us that it was too dangerous to come to find us as by this time there would be wild animals around! I remember my friend saying "ok, so it is too dangerous for anyone to rescue us, so I suppose that we had better stay here then ".

We began our day by wanting to see animals but now we were praying that we didn't see animals!

It was amazing that in the midst of such a dangerous situation that we all felt peaceful. The other problem was that we only had two bananas, a few sweets and 2 drinks between us and also, we were beginning to get cold as it can get cold at night in the mountains, and we had only gone with summer clothes thinking we were only on a day out. In hindsight it seems very foolish to have not gone prepared, but God was so amazing in the situation. So, we had to sleep in the car all night although I don't think any of us did much sleeping! I remember halfway through the night needing to go to the toilet and the Pastor panicking that I should not go far! I said, "I am not going far, just literally outside this door".

Eventually the dawn began to break, and we saw bright headlights coming towards us. It was a truck with people on it and the Pastor stopped the truck and began to explain our situation. Myself and my friend were then instructed to get on the truck and they would take us to the lodge that was located within the national park. I don't know which was worse, spending the night in the wilderness or bumping along on the back of the truck trying to hold on not to fall out. The locals are very used to travelling on the back of trucks but for a mzungu as they call us – it was a very challenging experience. However, we arrived safely and managed to check in to the lodge while the Pastor waited with the car for a mechanic.

I don't know how many angels were on assignment that night, but I am sure that there must have been many. We later heard that there was a herd of elephants a bit further up the hill that had pushed a lot of trees over in the night, but they had not come near us – hallelujah.

The lodge that we stayed in was beautiful and surrounded by the mountains and clear waterfalls and small deer that walked around and under normal circumstances it would have been wonderful, but we were just glad to all be safe. After showering and then realising that we had not even come with a change of underwear we made our way to have something to eat.

By this time the guest house that we had left in Chitipa were also trying to find out if we were ok as we hadn't returned the previous night. It is certainly an experience that I will never forget. I would like to return there again one day for memories but this time to travel in a proper 4/4 vehicle which is actually a necessity for most of the roads in Malawi. So many cars get destroyed because they are not suitable for the bumpy, pothole roads that you find in most places especially once you are outside of town.

We can now look back at this time and laugh and we have nicknamed it "the Nyika experience" as we were travelling through the Nyika national park.

The purpose for telling that story is to show how amazing the protection of God is when we trust in him, and I know that many people were praying for us that night.

I could share countless examples of when we have been protected on the roads but will just share one of them.

Puncture in Mzuzu

We had been preaching at a meeting in Mzimba and were on our way back to Mzuzu where I was staying in a hotel. Suddenly as we were travelling along, the car began to vibrate and shake, and I realised that a tyre had burst. The driver managed to safely slow the car and pull over but now we were in the dark and on a stretch of road that has very limited phone signal and the bishop and the driver are now outside inspecting the tyre with a torch while I am sitting inside the car. Now they try to find the spare tyre and also locate a Jack, which doesn't work. Jacks not working seems to be a very common problem in Africa. I have had many experiences by the side of the road with jacks that don't work and someone having to go off to find one somewhere. Anyway, the Jack won't work, and they can't find a way to lift the car so that they can replace the tyre, so they begin trying to flag down passing motorists to help us, but no one wants to stop because it is now dark, and people are afraid to stop. All this time I am praying and also sending messages through to the prayer team asking them to pray. The first miracle was that my wi fi was working!

Eventually a car with about 6 young men stopped and I could hear the bishop and the driver talking with them. The next minute these 6 young men lifted the car up with their hands while I am still sitting in it while the driver managed to change the tyre. What a miracle. I don't know if those men were men or if they were angels but all I know is that they were sent by God to help us.

As we continued safely on our way, I was thanking God for his protection and help. As I arrived back at the hotel I managed to arrive just before they were about to stop serving evening meals so managed to not only get back safely but to relax and enjoy a nice dinner as well. I was certainly very happy to see my hotel room that night!

Fuel crisis

Another testimony of Gods help and protection was when we had to travel across Malawi during the time of a fuel crisis. In 2022 Malawi experienced a bad fuel crisis where there was hardly any fuel in the country and half of what was available was being sold on the black market for double the cost of the normal price at the filling station. It did not seem like a sensible time to travel far north to the furthest point in Malawi but that was in fact what we did, and we saw the amazing provision of God all the way there and all the way back without needing to use black market fuel. We set off from Lilongwe having managed to fill the tank with fuel and were planning to spend the night at a guest house in Rumphi on our way to Chitipa but as we were nearing to Mzuzu, Cheryl the Pastor travelling with us from USA began looking at the fuel gauge and could see that we were not going to make it to Rumphi and that it was unlikely that we would find any petrol stations along the way selling fuel. We all made a decision that we would change our plans and spend a night in Mzuzu instead. We managed to reach Mzuzu with the fuel gauge on red and as we checked in to one of my favourite hotels, I remember standing in my room and thanking God for his goodness. We had reached Mzuzu safely, we were not stuck on the side of the road, but God had also brought us to one of my favourite hotels to stay in. While we refreshed and went to enjoy a nice evening meal together, our driver went to look for fuel and found that one of the petrol stations was expecting a delivery so decided to wait in the line. A few hours later, we got a phone call to say that he had managed to fill up the tank again and we were all set for starting off again the next day. Hallelujah!

After a very pleasant stay, we left after breakfast for the next journey up to Chitipa and as we were arriving in Chitipa the petrol station there was just receiving a delivery and we were first in the queue to fill up again for the return journey. In so many ways on that trip, we saw the provision of God helping us to go from one end of Malawi to the other.

When I needed to get to the south which was experiencing an even bigger fuel shortage, God provided in another way. The fuel shortage at this time was mostly petrol, but diesel could be found easier, so instead of a petrol car, now God provided for me to be taken in a diesel car. God always has a way of getting us where he needs us to be. In so many ways I saw the hand of God protecting and guiding us.

On this trip, I marvelled how we managed to travel the length of Malawi in the middle of a fuel crisis, but God is faithful.

Angels fix a car

I was being driven back from Balaka to lilongwe after a very successful month staying there where we had seen God doing miracles. Suddenly as we were passing along the border of Mozambique where there are a lot of hills, the car started making funny sounds and seemed to not be able to pull up the hills. I was praying and thinking that this would not be a good place to break down!

Eventually we managed to slowly make it to the next village where the driver pulled over to ask a mechanic to have a look at the car. We waited for about an hour while the mechanic pulled everything out but couldn't find the problem and then told us that the best thing is to try to reach the next main town to a garage. I was wondering how we would make it to the next main town of Dedza which involved going up steep hills and the car was struggling every time there was a hill. Anyway, the driver started up the car, but as he did so, I laid my hands on the dashboard and said, "In the name of Jesus, I command this car to work, and I ask for angels to fix this car and take us safely to our destination". As we set off, I suddenly noticed that now the car is not pulling or making funny noises and we are even racing up the hills without any problems. Everyone was amazed. When we reached to Dedza, the driver decided to still call at the garage and when the mechanic looked at the car, he just located one plug that was not in properly and just pushed it in and off we went, but the amazing thing was that the car had already been working before he pushed the plug in! It was like angels had held the plug in until we got to a safe place. After that we continued our journey all the way back to Lilongwe without any more problems. I thank God who sent angels to help us, so we were not stranded somewhere. Unlike in the west, there is no breakdown service. If you breakdown, you breakdown, and must find your own way out of the situation and if you are in a remote place, it is not easy, and sometimes people are stuck for more than a day, so we thank God for angels on assignment.

7. Miracles in Malawi

Miracles of healing and deliverance

There have been so many countless miracles of healing and deliverance that have taken place over the years that there would not be enough space to write them all. I remember one time when we were on an open-air meeting in Chitipa and so many people wanted to testify to healing and we didn't have time to hear them all because it was getting dark. So, I will try to just highlight some of the ones that stand out in my memory and hope that you will be encouraged that God is a God of wonders.

As I am writing I am reminded of the lady in one of the villages in the north of Malawi who had not been able to eat solid food for around 30 years as it would just cause her to be sick, so she survived all that time on very limited nutrition. She had visited hospitals and doctors all over Malawi but to no avail. In one of our meetings, she came forward for prayer and when I returned back a year later, she wanted to give her testimony that after receiving prayer, she went home and for the first time in 30 years was able to eat a proper solid meal and the same thing continued to happen ever since that day. What a mighty God we serve.

Hospital visits

On several occasions we have had the privilege of going into the local hospital in Chitipa and preaching the gospel and praying for the sick. The freedom to be able to proclaim the gospel is amazing and as I started preaching the whole ward including patients, visitors and staff listened to what I had to say and nearly everyone responded to receive Jesus and to receive prayer for healing. As we made our way around the ward praying at each bed, we later heard amazing testimonies of how many people had discharged themselves after prayer because they were healed. One man had a stroke and could not speak properly or move his right side of his body, but his family told us later that after prayer, the man got up and went home and was walking and talking normally.

Another lady had an issue of bleeding but in faith she reached out and touched my clothes like the woman with the issue of blood in the bible and immediately her bleeding stopped, and she went home.

We also went into the maternity ward where many women were due to have C Section due to complications but after prayer, we learnt that they all went for normal delivery. There was also a baby that was on a ventilator and was very seriously sick. We went to pray for the baby and then the next day one of the church elders went to follow up on the baby and didn't find him in the high dependency unit and so was fearing the worst that maybe he had died but then suddenly he was told that the baby had made an amazing recovery and was now with his mother on a normal ward.

We also had the opportunity to go into the baby's neo natal ward where the premature babies were and had the opportunity to pray over them and speak life into their little bodies.

Like a lot of places in Malawi the hospitals are very basic and lack even essential medicines and even the food for the patients must be brought in by their relatives and I also noticed that there were no mattresses or pillows on the beds either. So, we also took in gifts of basic necessities for the patients of toothbrushes and toothpaste and soap and even gave paracetamol tablets to the hospital staff as they were lacking even basic medicines. So, with all this in mind, it is not surprising that when someone comes with a message of hope, that they are willing to listen and respond to the offer for prayer and God heard the cry of their hearts with the amazing results that we saw.

One time we had to go to every ward preaching and praying for people and we did not have enough time to complete everywhere and people in other wards were complaining that we had not visited them. In fact, we heard an amazing testimony from the staff. Every morning they meet to discuss patients on their wards and what is happening and how many people have died and how many people have been discharged and they said that they noticed that on the wards that we had prayed on, nobody had died which was apparently very unusual. They then requested that we needed to go back the next day to speak in the other wards so we told them that we would visit the following afternoon after coming back from visiting one of the branch churches. However, the next day after leaving the branch church where it began to rain heavily, we went out to get in the car and found that the roads were now muddy and becoming impassable and not long down the road, our car got stuck in the mud and we ended up stuck for several hours while young men from the church tried to dig us out! So, unfortunately by the time we made it back to the town, it was too late to visit the hospital much to the disappointment of the people, but we promised to visit them another time.

In the church we regularly see pregnant women coming from the hospital to ask for prayer for safe deliveries and God touches them.

So, we saw that indeed God was doing amazing things beyond our understanding.

Another amazing situation that happened in Balaka in 2022 was when I was ministering in a church and my accommodation was within the church compound, so people would often turn up for prayer at all times. One morning I was awoken by the Pastor telling me that some ladies had brought another lady directly from the hospital as she was seriously sick with fever and could hardly breathe and the hospital had been unable to identify what was wrong with her. Upon entering the church office, I spoke with the lady and shared the gospel message with her, and she received Jesus in her life. We then began to pray for her for healing, at which point the lady began to vomit yellow fluid all over the floor but afterwards she was completely healed. She then went outside to walk around and found that she could now breathe normally and walk without any difficulty – hallelujah! She and the other ladies were amazed, and this set off a chain of events where every day people began coming from the hospital asking for prayer because word had gone around that Jesus is healing people at the church. It was certainly an exciting time wondering who would be turning up for prayer each day and every day we saw God doing miracles.

One older lady came to the office with severe back pains but after prayer she began to bend up and down without pain and was so amazed and grateful that she began crying and raising up her hands to the Lord. More about these miracles in Balaka in a later section but I wanted to include those few testimonies with the section on hospital visits.

So, sometimes we visited hospitals and sometimes people from hospitals came looking for us.

The chief gets healed.

One of the first miracles that I witnessed in Chitipa was on one of my first visits when the chief of the area got healed of leg pains that he had had for 8 years. For those who understand African culture, you will know that chiefs carry a lot of weight in the area and this man has become a blessing to the church and to our ministry. At the time I didn't know that he was the chief, but he came forward for prayer for healing because he had been suffering with pain in his leg for 8 years. As I prayed for him, all the pain left, and he was totally healed and is still healed to this day many years later. He then became a very committed member of the church and when it was time for me to buy the land for the women's refuge, he was very influential in giving me favour as a foreign national wishing to buy land which is not easy and was involved in the negotiations and transactions that took place without which it could have been a much harder process. After purchasing the initial piece of land, we were subsequently also offered 2 other pieces of land adjoining to the land at very cheap prices, and we are believing in the future that there will be a whole complex on that land for the glory of God. We have also referred to the compound as "Kingdom City" and are believing for a beautiful compound to be built there for the glory of God.

Another lady had been diagnosed with cancer by the hospital but after prayer she returned back to the hospital who told her that there was no trace of cancer in her body.

Another time there was a man who came for prayer because he had a motorbike accident and had damaged his leg and foot and 6 months later, he was still in pain. After prayer, God completely healed him and as he gave his testimony, one of the first things he said was "now I can play football again" as he began kicking his leg around without pain!

Many times, as we have prayed for people, I then ask them to do something that they couldn't do before, and we see people with leg and knee pains running around the church and people with back pains now bending up and down. People with frozen shoulders now lifting up their arms to worship God.

<u>The blind see</u>

One time we were having a large meeting where people were attending from also Zambia and Tanzania which border near to Chitipa. A group of people had brought a blind lady to the meeting and had come with her from Tanzania holding her by the hand because she was blind. After prayer the lady began to see and was able to follow me around the room unaided and went back to Tanzania rejoicing.

Another time we prayed for an older man who was blind and after prayer he began to see. I remember that on the following Sunday the church was so full it was standing room only at the back because so many people had come because they had heard about the blind man who began to see. One of the good things in Africa is that word spreads quickly due to their community style of living so when miracles begin happening, it is not long before a crowd begins to come to see what is happening. Everyone knows their neighbours unlike in the west.

Continuing on with testimonies of eyesight restored from the youngest to the oldest.

One time a group of students came forward for prayer because either they couldn't see long distance or short distance and were struggling at school to read properly.

Another thing I should mention is that obtaining glasses in the villages is not easy, so this is probably another reason why we see so many miracles of sight being restored. I actually wear glasses myself for distance and have often thought it strange that here I am praying for people's eyesight to be restored and then putting on my glasses!

Anyway, these students came forward and I prayed for them. Then someone took them to check if they could see better and each one testified that now they could either see further or read better! Hallelujah.

Another time we went to a village branch and God was doing miracles as usual and suddenly a 100-year-old lady came forward. 100 years old is almost unheard of in Malawi. They even consider you are old if you are over 50! So, this lady comes forward and says that she can't see properly which most people would think was normal, but I asked this lady, "do you believe that God can heal you?" And she said "Yes". So, I said "according to your faith, be it unto you". Afterwards I asked her how much she could see, and she went to the back of the church and told me that now she could see much better than before! Everyone was amazed that God would even heal a 100-year-old lady.

One one visit I saw so many miracles of God restoring sight mostly to those who maybe had conditions that are curable in the West like cataracts but in the villages, they don't even know what it is. They just tell you that they see like cloudiness over their eyes but many times God does his own surgery and removes the cataracts so they can see clearly again. One of the phrases from our recent trip was "now I can see clearly". God is opening up people's eyes both spiritually and physically in Jesus name.

In many villages people were healed of eyesight problems and then proceeded to walk around the church outside to test whether they could now see more than they could before and most of the time they could now see further than before.

We do also take out reading glasses for people which have been very popular, but it is so much better when God heals completely.

The deaf hear.

In the time of Jesus we read that the blind saw and the deaf heard and the lame walked. The bible says that Jesus Christ is the same, yesterday, today and forever and so I always encourage people that God is still doing miracles today and indeed we have seen this before our eyes every place that we go.

One time I called forward those that were deaf and not able to hear properly and 5 people responded. 4 of them could not

hear out of 1 ear and the other had problems hearing in both ears. As we prayed, God supernaturally opened up all of their ears instantly. It was the most amazing time as people shouted, clapped and jumped up and down in excitement at what God did. One lady gave a testimony that since childhood, she could not hear out of one ear, but she said that as I prayed, she felt like something coming out of her ear and now she could hear properly – hallelujah!
I even have a video that someone took of the testimony taking place and the whole congregation erupting in joy and me doing a little dance!

Every testimony is powerful but there are some that are so amazing that they cause something inside you to jump for joy. This testimony was one of them.

Another one that made me jump for joy was when a pregnant lady came for prayer telling me that the hospital said they could not hear any movement inside of her, so I prayed and spoke life back into the baby. She went back to the hospital for another check and now the baby was moving!

Another testimony that was amazing was a lady who had asked me to pray for her child who was having constant epileptic fits every day. Several times a day the mother would see the child having seizures. They came to the office, and I prayed for the child. As I was at the end of my time there, I left not knowing what had happened but when I returned a year later, the lady came to testify that since that time, her child had not had one single seizure – she was totally healed.

I love when I see instant healing, but I also love when I return back and hear these kinds of testimonies because it means that the healing has been lasting and has made a total transformation in someone's life.

Another time near Kasungu there was a lady who had a motorbike accident 2 years previous and had been left in pain when she walked, but after prayer she began running around the church totally free from pain.

In Balaka we saw countless miracles. Every day people would come to the office for prayer. One older lady came who was in so much pain in her back that she had strapped her back with cloths to try to ease the pain but after prayer she could bend up and down without pain and the amazement and joy on her face was incredible as she realised that Jesus had taken away her pain.

One time I was called to the office where 2 young ladies had come for prayer and wanted to tell me their stories. I then found out that the guest house next to the church was being used like a house for prostitutes and these young women were working as prostitutes but had tired of that life and wanted to stop doing it. Often you will find that women in Africa and indeed in a lot of places are not doing it because they enjoy doing it, but because of poverty and because they have no other options. These ladies shared that their family members had died, and they had been left alone in the village with no way of supporting or taking care of themselves, so they decided to come into town to try to find a way of surviving.

I shared with them about the Saviour who loved them and has a good plan for their lives, and they readily received Jesus into their lives. We then gave them some money for transport to go back to their village and connected them with pastors in their areas who could help them. We also spoke with them about things that they would like to do to be able to support themselves like starting small businesses so they could leave their old way behind and begin a new life. Like most places, it is hard to break a lifestyle and enter a new way but slowly we are changing lives one by one and on the following Sunday we were pleased to see them in church.

In Lilongwe where we conducted an open-air meeting in one of the poorer districts, we saw a lady who had just come from the hospital being healed. The lady was from out of town and had only come to Lilongwe to visit the hospital and then stay with her relatives who lived right near to where we were conducting the open air. In fact, during the meeting, she was not in attendance but was listening from the house but when I said that I was going to pray for the sick she decided to come out and stand in the prayer line and God healed her. God is so amazing that she came to Lilongwe to visit a hospital, but God had another plan of supernatural healing.

It is also encouraging because it goes to show that when you preach outside you never know who might be listening, not just the people who seem to be listening but through the P.A system the sound is going out all across the area. I remember one time in India when we were leaving the meeting and people began running out of their houses thanking us for the message. Due to a lot of persecution in India, many people were afraid to publicly attend the meeting, but many were still listening from their homes.

Sometimes we may never know the impact that we are making but as we preach and pray and listen and help, we are sowing seeds into people's lives that may sprout into a great harvest. I want to encourage you to never give up doing good because the bible says that at the appointed time, we will reap a harvest if we do not give up.

Building church in Uganda.

New church land for bible school and children's church in Uganda.

Joshua & Isaac - before and after photos

Women's refuge – Malawi

Typical African village toilet.

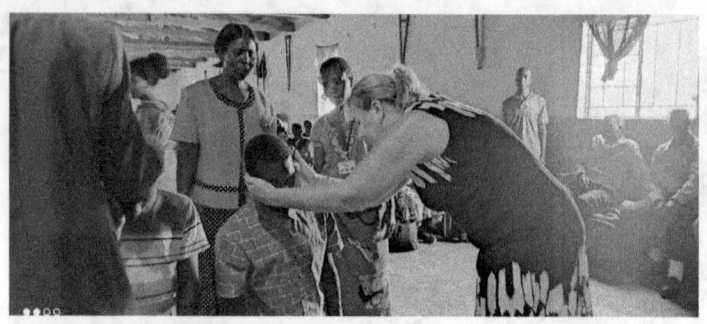

The deaf hear and the lame walk.

Revival meetings.

Man healed of leg pains after motorbike accident in Uganda

Giving gifts.

Assisting the survivors of cyclone Freddy.

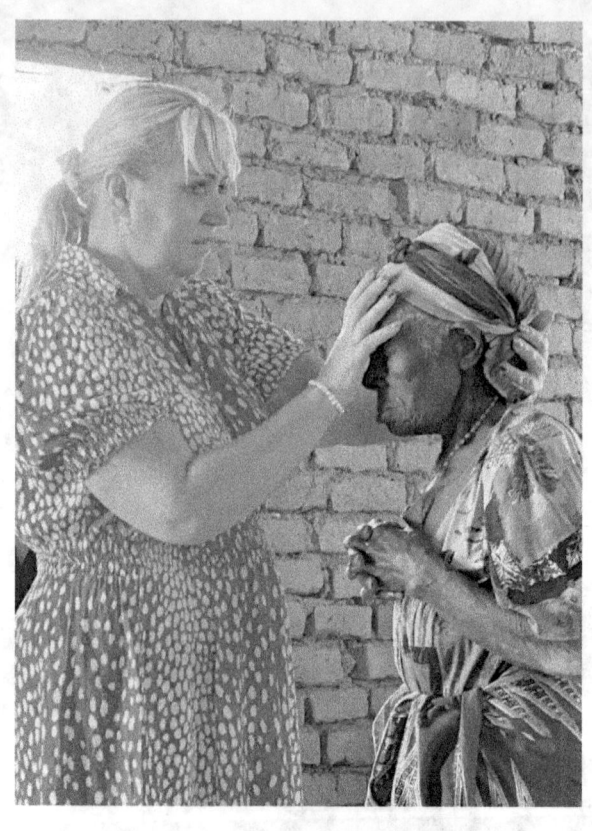

God moving in power.

Orphans in India.

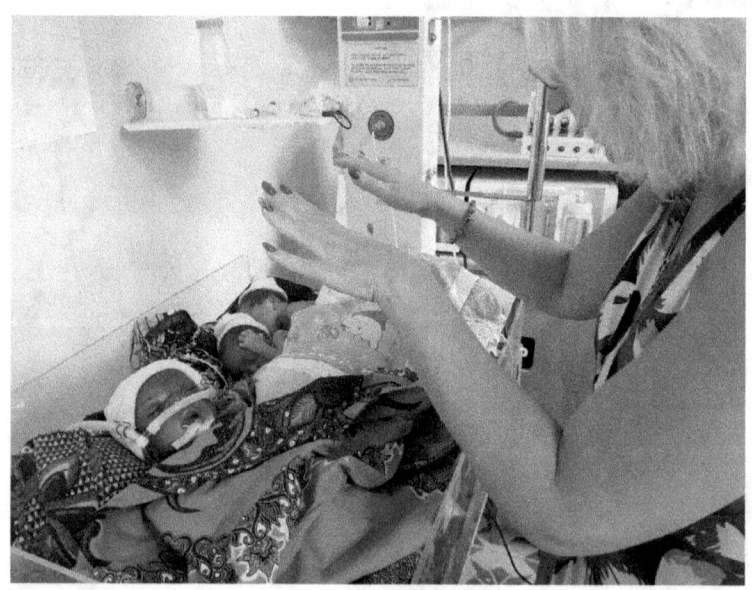

Praying at the hospital in Malawi.

Orphans in India receiving gifts.

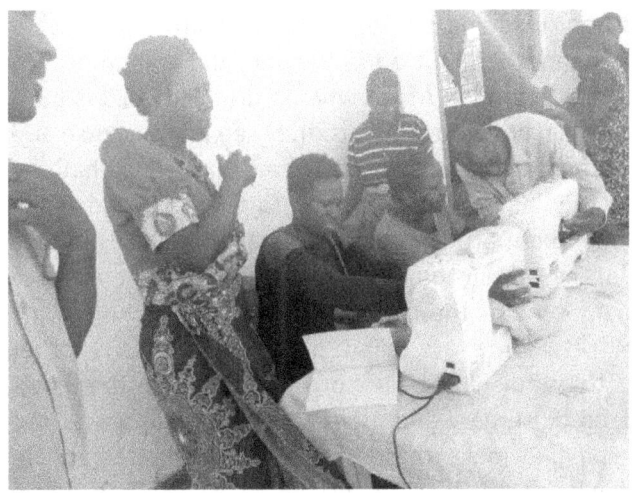

Women learning tailoring in Malawi.

8. Miracles in Uganda

Uganda was the very first African country that I visited apart from South Africa that I had visited previously. Over the past 13 years since I first visited Uganda, there have been so many lives that have been transformed but I will just try to remember a few testimonies to share with you. We usually begin our programme in Kampala, but also travel to other towns to minister in different churches and conferences.

One of the places that we have visited many times is a place called Kigumba which is about 4 hours' drive from Kampala. We have a friend there called Hugh who is from the UK but working out in Uganda running a children's project called "Jesus loves the little children", which helps disabled and vulnerable children with Jesus clubs, assistance with hospital fees and school fees and visiting with the guardians who are sometimes the mothers but often they are the grandmothers. There is a great stigma in Africa when a disabled child is born and because of their cultural beliefs, they see it like a curse and often the father will reject the child, even denying that the child is his. This leaves the mother with the child and if the mother wants to remarry and the new husband refuses to take on the child, then often the disabled children are left with the grandmother. Some of the children have cerebral palsy, some have club feet, some are blind or deaf and many other deformities that they have been born with. Some of the things can be helped by surgery and other things through prayer but Hugh is helping to make these children's lives better and to assist those who are taking care of them and giving them a safe place to come and meet together. It is also showing to the community that these disabled children have value rather than being cast aside.

This year we were able to be part of the Glory Kids meeting where they gather the children and their parents once a month at the church.

Through this connection, we were able to connect with the pastor of the church – Pastor Shadrach and have been many times to conduct conferences there and have seen the place change over the years. The first year that we visited we found that there was a very hard spiritual atmosphere but slowly over the years, we have seen God breaking through and this year we saw amazing miracles taking place.

I remember one time, as I was preaching, I saw a lady coming in at the back, not able to stand up straight and being assisted down the aisle by another lady. I waited to see what they were going to do as they continued walking towards me. They continued walking until they stood right in front of me wanting me to pray. I immediately sensed that there was a witchcraft curse over the lady that was causing her to not be able to stand up straight and walk. As I rebuke the curse of witchcraft, the woman fell down on the floor, but when she got back up, she was now standing straight and proceeded to run around the church and by this time the whole congregation were up on their feet cheering and clapping to the Lord for the great miracle that he had done – hallelujah!

In Africa I find that a lot of sicknesses are also connected to witchcraft and when you break that, the person is instantly healed.

On our recent visit, there was a lady who told me she had stabbing pains in her foot like a needle going in. I prayed for her, but the pain remained. So, then I asked her to sit down on a chair and as I held her foot in my hand, I then commanded every witchcraft curse to be broken and I pulled out of her foot every fiery dart of the enemy. As I did that, suddenly the pain left her and now she was able to walk freely without pain.

Baby Anna

Another miracle in Kigumba was a lady who came for prayer when she was pregnant and there was a problem with the pregnancy where the baby was laying the wrong way in the womb, but as we prayed, God did a miracle and turned the baby the right way around. I got a message after I got home from that trip to tell me that the lady had given birth naturally, the baby was healthy and that they had decided to name her after me because I had prayed for them, so the baby was called Anna. On this last trip I was privileged to meet Anna who is now 3 years old, and I prayed for Anna to grow up to be a woman of God and there was a wonderful presence of God as I prayed for Anna.

Over the years I have also had several women name their babies after me because I have prayed for them when they were barren and not able to conceive but after prayer they have managed to conceive and give birth to a healthy child. So, there are lots of baby Anna's all over Africa!

During our time at the conferences in Kigumba, we usually come back with many different gifts from the people showing their appreciation. Most of them cannot give you money, but they bring their gifts in the form of chickens, bananas, cassava, potatoes, rice, goats etc. I remember one time we drove all the way back to Kampala with 6 chickens tied on the roof rack with the suitcases. It is a great honour to receive gifts and the

African people are very hospitable and do their best to make a guest feel welcome. Whenever we arrive in Kigumba, we find the women lined up outside the church waiting to give us the official ululating greeting as we walk to the church as the honoured guests. They come so expectant to receive from the Lord and I believe that is one of the reasons why we see so many miracles. Hunger and expectation draw out the anointing.

During our visit in 2022 we saw some amazing miracles taking place and the one that stands out to me the most is the pastor who was healed of leg pains after a motorbike accident. As I was ministering, I asked all the pastors to come forward for prayer. As they were coming, I noticed one man walking with a stick. After the general prayer for ministry, this man then asked me to pray for him for healing. He had been in a motorbike accident a year ago and his friend had fallen off the bike and died but he had survived but was left with pain in his leg and couldn't walk without the stick. As I began to pray for him, God touched him in a mighty way, and he began to be able to lift up his leg and then he began to run around the church jumping up and down in excitement. He then came and fell down on his knees thanking God for what he had done. I have a photo of him kneeling down thanking God and me holding the stick that he didn't need any more – hallelujah! We serve a miracle working God.

Another meeting on our last trip, we saw several miracles in one meeting in Kampala. One lady who had tinnitus in her ears after testing her mother's hearing aids in her own ears received total healing. She told me that she had been looking after her mother and her mother was saying that the hearing aids were not working. So, she had put them in her own ears to test them and since that time, she had been left with horrible ringing in her ears. As I put my fingers on her ears and prayed, she then began shaking her head and saying, "I can't hear it", so I asked her what she couldn't hear? She then told me the story and how she had been having a horrible sound in her ear but now the sound had gone, and I could see from her face that she was amazed.

Another lady had a stroke and was in pain down one side, but after prayer the pain left. Another lady was not able to read properly but after prayer, we bought her a bible and she began to read and be able to see clearly. I remember at the end of that service, getting up and dancing on the platform giving praise to the Lord for the wonderful things that he had done. There was such an atmosphere of the presence of God and joy in that place that night.

Creative miracles

The bible says, "lay hands upon the sick and they will get well" and this we have seen many times. But there are also times when I have experienced angels walking into a meeting and people have received healing and creative miracles even without anyone laying hands on them.

This last trip in Uganda, I was in such a meeting. I suddenly sensed the atmosphere change, and I knew that angels had walked in the room. Then I heard the words "new lungs". I spoke out "someone needs new lungs". Then I heard a lady scream and fall down on the floor without anyone touching her. Later she got up and began to say that she was pregnant, but she had a lung condition and the hospital had told her that she would not be able to give birth naturally. She said that after getting up off the floor, that now she could breathe normally!

About a week later I heard that the lady had gone back to the hospital, and they had checked her over and found that now there was nothing wrong with her lungs and told her that now she will be able to give birth normally – hallelujah!

In the same meeting, I then asked people to place their hands on the part of their body where they needed healing. As they did so, one lady who had experienced pain in her head for 15 years since going to a hair salon where they had put some wrong chemicals on her head, placed her hands on her head. She said that as she placed her hands on her head while I was praying, she felt like cold water being poured on her head and then she found that all the pain had gone. 15 years of pain gone because Jesus reached out and touched her. Just like the woman in the bible with the issue of blood who reached out to touch Jesus – people around the world are still reaching out to touch Jesus and finding that their lives are being transformed.

I have also had experiences where I have seen angels walking in the meeting usually holding silver platters carrying body parts. In several meetings I have seen people receiving new kidneys.

People often think "can this really be true?" But I always say that it is God who created us in the beginning, and we are so wonderfully made, so if we need a new body part at some time, is it really too hard for the Lord who created everything, to bring a new body part?

Financial miracles

Not every miracle is about physical healing, there are many other breakthroughs that people receive through prayer. On this last trip I heard several testimonies of God bringing provision to people. One place I went a man testified that the previous year I had given him a prophecy about open doors. He had believed and stood on that word and over the course of that year God had done great things for him. He then pointed to the car park and said, "one of the breakthroughs is right there" and as I looked, I saw a beautiful 4/4 vehicle that God had blessed him with parked in the car park.

In the same meeting I prophesied over a lady concerning business and financial breakthrough. A few days later we were in another meeting and the husband of this lady came to testify. He told me that him and his wife had been running a project but due to covid and other economic problems, they had not received any donations for a long time and the project was going to close. He said that after his wife received that prophecy, that very same night someone sent them a large donation and they got the notification on their phone in the middle of the night! Glory to God. He is Jehovah Jireh, the Lord our provider and he knows exactly what we need and when we need it.

Prison ministry

During this trip we were also invited to preach in the local prison. Prisons in Africa are unlike in the West and the facilities are often limited and all the prisoners are housed together in like dormitory style just sleeping on the floor. They must also provide their own food by relatives bringing it for them. Most of them are also forced to do hard labour usually in the form of farming and digging. Despite the grim conditions, we also found that many of them had found faith in Jesus and were very open to hearing what we had to say. One time I was asked to pray for those that were due to attend court and I learnt later that everyone that I had prayed for had been acquitted and released. In the prisons that we have visited, they are mostly convicted of what we would call minor crimes or even what in the west we would consider a civil case like land disputes, or not fulfilling to pay dowry for a marriage or cases like stealing a goat. Obviously, there are many in prison for serious offences but the places that we have visited have tended to hold the low-level offenders. I remember visiting one prison in Chitipa and I thought I was in the middle of a revival as they all began shouting hallelujah as I was preaching and around 90 prisoners stood up to receive the Lord.

So, in Kigumba we began a service of worship and then I shared the word about the Prodigal Son repenting and coming home to the father, and how the father was not standing to condemn him but to welcome him with open arms. As they heard about the love of the Father waiting to welcome them home if they would turn from their old ways, many raised up their hands to receive Jesus. I then prayed for those who needed healing, and many began to testify that pain that had left their body. One man said he had fallen out of a tree and his back had been hurting for 7 years, but that day, all the pain left. Another man said that he had pain all across the back of his shoulders, but after prayer, all the pain left. Many were rejoicing because of the love of God who shows mercy and kindness and the offer of new beginnings.

While the service was taking place, I noticed that there were several baskets behind us of different sizes that the prisoners had made and were selling to make some income for their needs. As I looked at them, I had in mind that I would buy one before I left. As we were preparing to leave, suddenly one of the prisoners who was in charge of the prison church, asked me to just wait a few minutes. He ran off somewhere and came back carrying a beautiful basket with a lid on it and presented it to me and said that as a church, they would like to give me this as a gift. The pastor who was with us, looked at me in amazement and said that they have been visiting that prison for years and no one has ever received a gift before. I was very honoured to receive the basket as a sign of their appreciation of the amazing things that God had done that day. I have decided to use it as an offering basket and the couple travelling with me brought it back to the UK with them as they were leaving earlier than me and they took it back to our church, told the story of the basket, prayed over it and then took an offering in it and sent it to me to use for the rest of my trip in Uganda.

Another prison that we visited was near Balaka in Malawi which was run by Prison Fellowship as a half-way house when prisoners were nearing the end of their sentence and for those who were deemed to be reforming and open to faith in God. They work with the prison service but have a more relaxed atmosphere where the prisoners are able to learn skills to equip them for release. They have regular morning services and prayers and on one of these services, I was invited to preach where many people responded to the Lord. Afterwards I stayed for several hours offering prayer and counselling in the chapel and one after another came to share their stories and ask for prayer. There were both men and women at this facility and all of them were wanting to turn their lives around when they were released. It is hard if they have no proper home or family to go to and no way of making a living after release so this facility is really trying to equip and teach them and on my way to Balaka we stopped to look at a piece of land in Lilongwe where they are hoping to be able to build another Prison Fellowship facility as the one near Balaka is the only facility to cover the whole of Malawi. It was very interesting to see the work that they are doing and how they are transforming lives.

9. Cyclone Freddy 2023

Cyclone Freddy was the longest lasting tropical cyclone ever recorded and travelled across the Southern Indian Ocean for more than five weeks during February and March of 2023 bringing devastation wherever it went. It affected Malawi, Mozambique, Madagascar and Zimbabwe.

I was in Uganda at the time when I began to hear reports about the devastation that was taking place in Malawi especially in the southern region and thousands of people had lost their homes, their possessions and some had even lost their lives and their loved ones.

Malawi is listed as one of the poorest countries in the world and many of their buildings are not built to withstand such storms, being built mainly of mud and water and many are also built on the side of mountains and as the rain was sweeping down the mountains, it was washing away people's homes along the way. Those who survived were just left with the clothes that they were standing up in. Many mourned the loss of loved ones including many children that were brought out of the rivers dead. Many died in mudslides that came down the mountains burying people in its path. Many were swept away by the fast flowing rivers, many were killed as their houses collapsed on them. Roads were destroyed and it became almost impossible to reach those who were in the villages. Crops were also destroyed, meaning a lack of harvest this year and more starvation and also causing high food prices due to the scarcity of maize.

The situation was devastating, and the aid agencies on the ground were not able to cope although I was surprised that it did not create much worldwide attention and was rarely seen on the world news which meant that the help that came was very limited.

Upon hearing of this devastation, our ministry leapt into action with the limited resources that we had, but people began to give generously towards an emergency appeal. Pastor Clement was able to go into some of the villages that had been affected and to take emergency supplies of essential food items, as well as bedding and pots and pans to assist the people with their immediate needs. Many of the villages that were being visited were predominantly Muslim and it was also an opportunity to share the gospel with these people and many received the Lord during this time. Pastor Clement was reporting back that the people were so pleased to see him, especially as many places had received no help at all until he came. He spent many nights sleeping out in the villages so he could bring some comfort to the people during that time. Every day I was hearing that many other villages were calling for him to come and also assist them, but we were limited on how much resources we could offer so many did not receive any help at all.

In every village there were thousands of people waiting to receive help, mostly forgotten by the world but not forgotten by God. Every day I was receiving photos of Pastor Clement preaching to thousands while handing out mattresses, maize, plastic cooking materials and other essential items just to try to show them that God had not forgotten them.

Local halls and schools that were still standing opened up to allow the displaced and homeless to sleep there and the Red Cross set up camps for those who had lost everything.

Several months on the rains have cleared but the devastation remains as many are unable to rebuild their homes and gain back their possessions in a country that is already ravished by poverty. The other problem is that cyclones in this part of the world seem to be an annual occurrence although this was the worst one the country had experienced, so even if they rebuild their homes, they cannot afford to build them to the standard to withstand another storm, so Malawi has many displaced people at this time.

A few years back, another cyclone hit the country and one lady Pastor who we are now supporting had part of the walls of her house knocked down which resulted in one of her children being killed. After the storm had gone, she tried to rebuild her house, but we decided that it would not be safe and the same thing could happen again another time, so instead we began to support her to rent a more stable home somewhere else. Even though she is safe for now, nothing can ever bring back the loss of her child and the trauma of that night.

Malawi right now is in a mess, but God is the one who can turn all things around for good and we pray that out of hopelessness and despair that God can bring hope and restoration.

10. India

India is a diverse country of cultures and religions, and the people worship many different gods so taking the gospel into India cannot be done effectively without the evidence of signs and wonders to demonstrate that Jesus is the one and true God who can save and heal.

One time we went right in the south to a town called Madurai, which is translated as the city of temples. People go to the temple to sacrifice to their gods and to ask for favour from the gods often taking with them items of food as their sacrifice to the gods. We were able to go with the good news that Jesus has become the one and only sacrifice that is needed and when the truth of that really comes to people, it is total freedom to their lives.

India is also a country of colours and noise and I remember on our first visit to Rajhamundry in Andrea Pradash, the sound of constant hooting of horns outside our hotel. It can at times seem very chaotic with a lot of people and animals walking in the road and the smell of spices everywhere. Driving takes on another dimension completely compared to back home. There didn't seem to be a side of the road for driving although I am sure by law there is! But they seem to drive wherever there is a space to get through while hooting their horns and trying to avoid other vehicles, animals and carts and people and anything else that happened to be on the road. Cows of course are considered sacred in India, so if they are in the middle of the road, you are not allowed to push them out of the way but must wait for them to move! We even saw elephants being transported on the back of lorries!

The women were dressed in traditional Sari with very exotic and vibrant colours especially in the northern and central regions of India. I remember when we went further south one time though, that the dress changed to more western dressing. One time the church decided that we should all wear traditional Sari costume for the Sunday service and so we were taken to the fabric shop to choose some fabrics and then taken to the tailors for fitting for the undergarment that goes under the long piece of cloth. We were measured and all measurements were taken and then on Sunday they came with our outfits for us to put on for Sunday service and to my horror I found that mine was too small! Even though we had been to the tailors for measurements, so I don't know what had happened (I certainly hadn't eaten enough in a few days to change the measurements!), but there was then a big panic as to what to do. I suggested that I just wear a T Shirt under it instead, but they were horrified at that idea and proceeded to try to unpick the stitching to make the undergarment bigger! I can't remember exactly what happened in the end, but we did arrive at church in our traditional dress much to the delight of the church. People abroad always love it when you show an interest in their culture either by eating their food or wearing their dress and especially if you can speak a few words of their language which I am not that good at I have to admit.

Another thing in India of course is curry. Curry for breakfast, curry for lunch, curry for dinner and with lots of spices. I don't mind a curry, but I am not a fan of spicy food and normally go for a mild chicken Korma back in the U.K so this also became an issue. I remember on the plane on the way out, they came around with the meal choice of curry or curry! I asked which one was the mildest and the stewardess said to me "you are going to India you know!". One time I remember asking the pastor if I could have the meal without spices and he assured me that "no spices", but when it came it was as hot as I could manage so I don't know what happened to no spices!

Coming downstairs for breakfast in the hotel, we began to look through the dishes on offer at the buffet and found nearly everything was Indian food until eventually we found boiled eggs so suffice to say, most mornings breakfast was boiled eggs and some bread. I found that they are also a fan of putting lots of sugar in their drinks which I then told them was contributing to a lot of diabetes as I found a lot of people were coming forward for prayer for diabetes which they called "sugar". One time the pastor went into a café to get me a cup of coffee and when I tasted it, it tasted like a cup of sugar. I don't take sugar in my drinks, so I said "Uhh, it has sugar in it" and the pastor said "yes, very nice"! I said "no, not very nice!". One time after church, they wanted to go for pizza and again even the pizzas had spices added to them although we did manage to find something that was ok. So, India has a lot of challenges for those coming from the west who don't like spices, noise and chaos but it also carries a lot of blessings as the people's hearts are open to hear and receive the truth.

We have travelled several times to India over the years and I remember on one trip, after I had preached a man came to ask me to pray for his arm that had been injured playing sports. I began by asking the man if he knew Jesus and he said that he did not. Then I asked him if he would like to know Jesus, but he declined and continued to ask me to pray for him to be healed. At this point I knew exactly what he was doing. He wanted to know – is your Jesus any different to all the other gods? He wanted to know that Jesus was real before committing his life to him. So, I prayed that God would heal him and also reveal himself to him. The man was instantly healed and then said that he now wanted to receive Jesus! Hallelujah.

In many of the meetings I would ask the Lord for a word of knowledge about healing, and I remember in one meeting asking for everyone who had back pain to stand up (not exactly a word of knowledge as there are sure to be many with back pains but that is what God told me to do as a demonstration of his power). So, every person with back pain stood up and I prayed and released healing from the platform and many people testified to pain leaving their body. After that I began to preach the gospel and found that there was now a greater openness to people listening to what I was saying as they had seen a demonstration of the power of God.

One time during a conference, we had taken a break for lunch and were in the pastor's house eating lunch when suddenly we were told that there was a queue of people outside waiting to see us to receive prayer. It reminded me of how the people in the bible used to run to wherever Jesus was. This is a hunger that we don't see in the U.K at the moment but let's pray that it will change. Another time after we had conducted an open-air meeting, we were trying to get into the car to leave and people were running along the side of the car trying to ask us to pray for them. Many countries around the world have a hunger for God that we don't see in the west at the moment. I remember in Malawi people waiting on the side of the road for us to leave our hotel in the morning so they could ask us for prayer. Many have no other hope, so they easily reach out in faith to the Lord just like the people in the bible who reached out to even touch the hem of Jesus garment to be healed. I believe that God sees such faith and honours them.

Sometimes you find that the women are very open to the gospel message but because of fear, they are reluctant to make a public confession. One time when we were leaving from an open-air meeting, we found that lots of women began running out of their homes, wanting to shake our hand and thank us for the message. We realised that they had not been in the actual meeting but because it was outside with a public PA system, they had been able to hear the word from their homes and had obviously made a secret confession of their faith in their homes. Many times, we may never realise the impact that we may have had on people or how many people have heard our words even without us realising. I remember hearing once about a preacher who used to go out into the woods to preach to the trees. He didn't think that anyone was listening. Some years later, a man came to see him and thanked him for sharing the gospel with him. The preacher asked him where he had heard him preaching and the man said that he was behind a tree listening when the preacher was preaching in the woods. That day, the man gave his life to the Lord and went on to do great things for the Lord. So, we should never give up preaching even when it looks like no one is listening because you just never know who is listening!

Another one of the challenges of preaching in India is that because they have so many gods, there can be a misunderstanding of just adding Jesus to the list of their many gods so for the pastors following up people it can be a challenge but the pastors there are doing an amazing job in a challenging situation and people's lives are being transformed.

Open doors

One time when we were in India God used a situation that happened to speak to me about a prophetic word of what he wanted to do in the lives of the pastors where I was just about to go to speak at a Pastors conference. I was waiting for the pastor to pick us up and I had gathered my things and come out of my hotel room to wait in the hotel foyer. Then I suddenly remembered that I had forgotten something so I went back to the room but after putting my key in the door, I found that it would not open. When the pastor arrived, I told him that the door would not open, so he took the key and tried, but it would still not open. Then he said that he would go to find the hotel manager who also came and tried, but still the door would not open so they said that they would call the maintenance man. The pastor and the hotel manager then went off to find the maintenance man while I remained sitting near my hotel room with the keys on the table. As I waited, I began to look at the keys and I heard the Lord say, "take the keys and open the door". I began to argue with God, that how can I open the door when I was the one who first reported that it wouldn't open! So, I remained sitting and waiting. Then I heard the Lord again saying, "I told you to take the keys and open the door". So, this time I picked up the keys and as I began to wiggle the key around, I suddenly heard a sound like something going back into place and then the door opened so fast that I flew through it and shouted, "the door has opened "just as the pastor was coming back up the stairs and I was shouting "pastor, the door has opened". I knew that God was showing me something supernatural and as I went to the Pastors conference, I relayed this story and told them, that when they went back to their villages, what they couldn't do the first time, if they would try again, the door would open for them. Then I prayed for them to receive the keys of the Kingdom to go back to their churches and do great things.

I have used this story around the world of how God will give us keys to open doors, even ones that would not open the first time. As I sensed that clicking, it was like a shift of alignment and sometimes God has to shift and align things in our lives in order for us to get the breakthrough that we are looking for.

In India, they also have a custom of taking off their shoes at the door and many places they still sit with women on one side and the men on the other side although of course for us as western visitors it was different, but they still expected us to take our shoes off on the platform so most of the time I preached in bare feet.

Child sponsorship Programme

Over the past few years, we have been supporting Pastor Solomon who runs a house with orphans, and they are housed and educated and brought into a family environment where they can flourish. To date, he is assisting 11 children, and we support some of them through a sponsorship programme where people give £30 a month which goes towards their education, food and clothing and other essential items that they need. Every month I receive regular updates and photos of the children receiving school books, or shoes or bags or sweets and fruit. The children are always nicely dressed and smiling, and they are being brought up in a Christian environment and many times you see the children kneeling in prayer or raising their hands up to the Lord, which is so encouraging to see. We are hoping that soon more of these children can receive sponsors.

India testimonies

As it was over 10 years ago since visiting India, I cannot recall all of the miracles that happened, but I have a sheet of paper that was given to me by the Pastor listing some of the people and the miracles that took place at that time so will name a few just as an encouragement of what God did.

1. Gurrayya – an old man healed of pain in his arm that he was suffering with for one year after being in a fight.
2. Seetharathnam – lady whose sight was wonderfully restored.
3. Varamma – lady healed of knee pains.
4. Chandramma – old lady healed of arthritis.
5. Verraju – man healed of problem in spine and and neck.
6. Moshe – man healed of asthma and lung problems.
7. Bushanam – man set free from smoking and other addictions.
8. Manga – healed of chest pains.
9. Jaya – lady healed of high blood pressure and diabetes.
10. Miriam – healed of ear and nose problems.
11. Nookalamma – healed of thyroid problems.
12. Parvathi – healed of spinal problems.
13. Dayamani – healed of abdomen pain in the womb.

These are just a small selection of the things that God while we were in India, but God was demonstrating his power and revealing who he is to the people.

11. Pakistan

Although we have not actually been to Pakistan, one of our members is involved with ministering to a ministry out there via zoom through Pastor Jamal and has seen some amazing miracles of healing over the internet and supports him and his team as they travel to the rural villages to minister to the Hindu tribes in what is predominantly a Muslim country.

The opportunities that are open to us at this time through the forum of zoom, Facebook, you tube, and many other similar platforms is amazing and although a lot of these social media may be used for evil, they can also be used for good and for spreading the gospel around the world.

For me the time of Covid 19 was also the time that God opened up to me the possibilities of reaching far more people through technology. I don't believe that technology should ever replace face to face meetings. Indeed there are a lot of places that will never be reached through the internet as many In countries like Africa and India don't have access to the internet especially in the villages although I have been surprised how many meetings I have been able to live zoom from the back of beyond villages in Africa allowing people back home to see what was going on which is amazing. One lady exclaimed "we saw miracles right in front of our eyes from our living room.

For me, I found that starting zoom meetings during Covid opened up a whole new online fellowship that is still running today as the people had bonded together over that time and asked me to continue on running the meetings even long after Covid was finished which was amazing.

So, it was during this time that we made connections with Pastor Jamal and began to follow the work he was doing and coming online to preach to the villages that he was going to. Seeing all the people in Pakistan sitting on the ground in their villages and people able to speak to them from our home all the way in U.K was quite incredible. Then as words of knowledge would be given, people would stand up to receive prayer and later testify to the goodness of God healing them.

Pastor Jamal has a vision not only to reach many villages with the gospel but also to establish schools and workshops to educate the local people.

Both India and Pakistan operate a caste system where some are considered untouchables and not given much opportunity in life. Some children are exploited and used as brick kiln workers to pay off the debts of their families, others are made to work in sweat shops or as maids or to search on the rubbish dump to find a few things to make a living. Giving these people an education and training them to do something can help to lift them out of poverty and suffering in their lives.

I notice that all across the poorer countries, people value education a lot more than in the west as they see it as their way out of poverty.

12. The Adventure Continues

<u>November 2023</u>

Today is 3rd November 2023, as I sit in the business lounge having just arrived in Nairobi and waiting to connect to Lilongwe in Malawi for another 5 weeks of ministry. Looking forward to reconnecting with friends across the country and seeing what God is going to do this time.

I left the U.K on a day when a storm was hitting the country with rain and high winds, but God was so faithful that London was not badly affected and after checking in all bags with a visit to the oversize department as usual, the flight took off for Nairobi arriving in the early hours of this morning. This chapter will aim to be an up-to-date report of what God is doing, and I hope that there will be many amazing testimonies to share with you in this part of the book.

After arriving in Lilongwe, I checked into a hotel for the weekend to rest and recuperate after the long journey before making the 4-hour journey down to Balaka on Monday. This was the place where I saw so many amazing miracles last year, so I am expectant of what God is going to do again this year. I met up with my friends Pastor Cheryl and Anita from USA who I travelled with last time and it was a blessing to reconnect and hear everything that God has been doing since I last saw them. Divine connections are a blessing in the body of Christ, and it was a joy to share ministry with them again these past few days. After arriving on the Monday afternoon, we rested before setting off for one of the villages on the Tuesday and the Wednesday. The bishop here has 65 branches, so there is always a church to visit on any day of the week. I remember that last year we visited many branches during the several weeks that I was here, and it is so amazing to see how far out into the bush, the word is being preached and churches are being established. Some of the roads that you go down, you begin to wonder if this is really a road and when you look around you only see trees and a few houses, so it is always very surprising when you finally arrive at the church and find a large number of people have gathered and you wonder where they have all come from and where they all live!

As we arrived at the branch church on Tuesday, we were met with an amazing group of singing women and children who had seen our car in the distance and had walked down the road to meet us and give us the traditional African welcome. What an honour as they followed the car up to the church while singing and welcoming us. In many of these villages, they may not get many visitors, especially ones from abroad, so they become very excited when they see that people have come all the way from the U.K and USA to visit them way out in the bush. Their expectation level is already high, and I believe that God responds to their expectation. All this week I have been battling with a cold that has been affecting my throat and was wondering how I was going to preach but just decided by faith that I was going to speak, and God supernaturally enabled me to speak despite what was going on with my throat. I spoke on how people reached out to Jesus in the bible to receive their miracle and I encouraged the people gathered to reach out by faith to receive whatever they were believing for. That day around 50 people responded to receive Jesus in their life and then I began to pray for the sick. Many testified to healing in their lives including a man who had arthritis in his leg but after prayer, he began to move his leg without pain. Others testified that they were having pains in their heart, but after prayer all the pain left. Others testified that pains in their head had been healed and we then prayed for a man who had a stroke, and the left side of his body was paralysed. After prayer, he testified that he could begin to see a change in his body, so we are believing that God began a work in his life that day. One thing that I have noticed is that sometimes healing is instant but sometimes it is a gradual process, and we should never be discouraged if it looks like nothing has happened because when we pray by faith, something always happens. The church is in the process of buying the land and will begin to mould their own bricks to make a structure for the church so it will be interesting to see the progress of this church when I come back another time.

On Wednesday we travelled again to another village that took nearly 2 hours on bumpy roads. I am glad that I don't get travel sickness! So, after what seemed like forever, we pull up outside a church building and are greeted by the pastor and leaders and some of the church congregation. Inside the worship team were leading in very exuberant worship. The Lord had laid on my heart to speak about the friends who had carried the paralysed man to Jesus and had lowered him through the roof and also the story in John 5 where the paralysed man sat by the pool at Bethesda, and when Jesus asked him if he wanted to get well, he replied that he had no one to help him get into the pool. I then encouraged the people that in life, we need divine connections, we need favour with God and with man if we are going to achieve anything in life. The man in the first story had friends that helped him but the man by the pool said that he had no one to help him which is a very sad place to be in life when we have no one to help us. That day around 30 people came forward to receive Jesus in their life and I also prophesied over a couple in the church concerning God blessing their marriage and the Pastor told me later that they had been experiencing problems for a long time, so I hope that they have now been encouraged and that God will help them with their situations.

On the way back from this church, the Pastor began to tell me a testimony of a couple that I had prophesied over the previous year when we went to Blantyre. I remember that I felt very strongly that I needed to go to Blantyre and as soon as we got in the meeting, I noticed a certain man who stood out. I began to prophesy about his business and how he had lost money through people betraying him, but God was going to remove those people and restore everything to him. Apparently, not long after that, the man testified that in fact everything I said happened and he got back everything he lost and more and that also his wife had been healed in that same meeting as well. It is always so encouraging when you hear the results of things that happened last time as well as the things that are currently happening.

As I write now, Malawi is going through another crisis, with the value of their currency going down 44% overnight causing the price of everyday commodities to double immediately which is going to cause a lot of pain and suffering for the people of Malawi who already live in one of the poorest countries on earth. I believe that God has brought us here for such a time as this to bring a message of hope to the people. Their currency has devalued several times over the past 2 years, but 44% is the biggest overnight drop that I have ever seen and only God can help the people of Malawi at this time.

On Thursday we began 2-day revival healing meetings at the main church here in town and I preached on God bringing freedom to his people and I plan to continue tonight with how the plagues in the book of Exodus did not touch the people of God, to encourage the people that even in the midst of this financial crisis, God can still supernaturally provide for his people who trust him in the midst of trouble. I also prophesied and prayed that God was breaking the spirit of delay in people's lives. In the same way that the world can cause things to happen overnight, so also God can move in our lives suddenly when it is his time. I then began to pray for the sick and many testified to healing in their lives. One lady had an accident falling off a bicycle and breaking bones in her ankle which left her walking with pain. After prayer, she said that it felt a lot better, and she was able to walk across the church without pain – hallelujah! Others testified to pain in their arms leaving and pain in their head leaving.

I am now sitting here listening to the worship band warming up in the church while there is a thunderstorm outside which is not a good thing when a service in Africa is about to begin, as most people don't have cars and they walk to church, so heavy rain often seriously delays and affects the attendance at church as people are reluctant to come walking to church in heavy rain. I am praying that this rain will now stop so that all those who want to attend the service today will be able to come. We are now the middle of November and approaching to the rainy season which then makes ministry very difficult especially for village ministry where roads become impassable. Today I only have to walk next door to the church, but the challenge is the people attending so may God stop this rain now in Jesus name.

After some delay, the service began, and God moved powerfully touching people's lives and healing and delivering them. One lady who had pain in her feet for several years and was finding it hard to walk properly, began to run across the church after prayer. Another man gave a testimony from the previous night that God had blessed his business and that day he had sold more fish than ever before, and all this was on the same day that Malawi had announced the devaluation of their economy. As I preached this night, I encouraged the people that God is faithful and that he makes a distinction between his people and the people that do not know him. In the book of Exodus when God was sending the plagues on Egypt, it says that in all the places where the people of God stayed, there was no plague. I encouraged them that though they may see a lot of uncertainty around them, that God will sustain them if they trust in him.

Another lady testified that she had had pain in her arm for 3 months and found it hard to do her farming but after prayer, she was feeling fine.

The next day I travelled back to Lilongwe and preached at a large church in town on the Sunday where 34 people gave their lives to the Lord which is the biggest miracle of all to see people coming to the Lord.

I am now waiting for another person from the UK to arrive before we begin proceeding north to Chitipa on the next section of this trip. I am excited to see what God is going to do in the next part of this trip as we tour around the north of the country before coming back down to Lilongwe again. We have a 3-day conference planned in Chitipa with many branches also coming together and I am excited to see what God is going to do. We will also visit the women's refuge and see the progress of what is taking place there.

13. Going to Chitipa

Today we begin our journey to Chitipa which is a 12-hour journey along roads with potholes and mountain passes. I often say that if it was not for the amazing things that I see once I get here, I would not make this journey but because of the amazing atmosphere and miracles that I see once I get here, I make the sacrifice to come. We are driven to our halfway point in Mzuzu and stay overnight before proceeding to Chitipa the next day.

We are picked up by the Bishop and driven the next 6 hours to Chitipa which takes us around some mountain passes where we often stop to feed the monkeys with bananas and where there are spectacular views of the lake below but it is also a dangerous place and the big trucks that are bringing supplies and fuel from the border of Tanzania have to pass that way as it is the only road from the North and they often get stuck on the steep hills which can cause the whole road to become blocked. In a country with no breakdown service, this can cause a huge problem with a truck stuck blocking the road for even 2 days! We met several trucks that had broken down or were stuck trying to get up the hills but by the grace of God we managed to find enough room to pass by and got through the mountain area.

We have arrived in Chitipa and waiting to see what God is going to do this time.

Chitipa Conference
17-19 November 2023

We begin on Friday with a leader's session where I teach about the importance of prayer and spending time in the presence of God. Sometimes leaders in Africa can be so busy trying to attend to everyone's needs as well as providing for their families in a country where it is hard for most Pastors to make a living out of ministry, so sometimes it is difficult to find a quiet time to seek the Lord. The Pastors here are very dedicated to the work of God but often circumstances make life very difficult for them.

In the afternoon and evening we had general sessions and God began moving powerfully by his Spirit and we saw lot of people responding to the gospel and receiving salvation as well as many healings and deliverances that were taking place. One lady responded to a word about leg pains which she said had just started suddenly. As we prayed for her, she was delivered from the pain and began walking across the room without pain. Others testified that heart problems had been healed and many other conditions were healed.

In the evening session, I wanted to also zoom the meeting live to people back home so they could see the wonderful things that God was doing but when I got to the church, I found that the lighting was not very good and the screen that was being filmed was very dark and people back home were not able to see clearly what was happening. I mentioned to the Pastor that people were trying to watch but they couldn't see anything clearly and were becoming frustrated, so he sent some men from the church to go and borrow some bigger lights and just as I was starting to talk, they came in with 2 big bulbs and a table and proceeded to stand on the table and change the light bulbs while I was waiting to preach! However, after replacing the smaller light bulbs with these big ones, it made a huge difference to the light in the building and now people were able to see clearly what was happening. I then proceeded to use this illustration in my message concerning how Jesus is the light of the world and how often we walk in darkness not knowing the direction that we are going, we cannot see clearly what God is doing but when light comes, everything becomes clearer. After the message several people responded to receive Jesus.

Before going to the meeting, I was praying and asking the Lord what he wanted to do that night and I heard him say "Today I am healing eyes", so halfway through my message, I shared that word and then asked everyone who was experiencing problems with their eyes to come forward. Quite a few people responded to the word, and I began to pray healing over their eyes. God began healing people and not long after the prayer, a whole line of people began to come to testify that God had healed their eyes. One lady testified that from birth she had been experiencing pain in one of her eyes and also that had caused her to not be able to see properly out of her eye but after prayer, she said all the pain went and now she could see clearly! Hallelujah.

Others testified to itching and scratching in their eyes being healed and near sightedness being healed. One lady said that she struggled to read properly, but after prayer, she went to the back of the church and was given a book to read and found that she could read it clearly. Another lady testified that she had been experiencing tears running from her eyes but after prayer, the tears had stopped. So many testimonies of God healing eyes last night. I have discovered something – always move with what God is doing. When God told me that he was healing eyes last night, I just moved into alignment with what he had already planned and then the miracles began happening.

After this, I continued preaching and then called people for salvation and then for more healing and again the testimonies flowed. One lady testified that she had a swelling in her breast but after prayer all the swelling had gone. Others testified to pain leaving from their stomach and head pains healed, a couple of ladies testified to being healed of pneumonia and there was also a lot of deliverance that began to take place as well.

We came back to our hotel rejoicing that indeed God is a miracle working God.

During our time here, we spoke to a lady working for an organisation teaching about nutrition. This is a much needed ministry as many do not understand the benefits of fruits and vegetables and even though you see an abundance of mangoes by the side of the road, they were never offered on the menu while we were in Chitipa and I had to ask the pastor to buy them for me at the market and then ask the restaurant to cut them up to accompany my breakfast. I try my best especially at home to take lots of fruits and so to just be presented with egg and chips and bread every morning is not good for you. So, I found avocados and mangoes and bananas and combined them with my breakfast. Mangoes in UK are a luxury fruit and expensive because it must be imported but here in this season, they are so cheap and yet many don't see the benefits apart from selling them. Therefore, I applaud those who are teaching about nutrition. Many are poor and can't afford certain foods or they are not available but fruits in the villages are cheap and in abundance, so it is just a matter of eduction of their benefits. The staple food here is Nsima which is a maize meal, and most

Malawians like to eat it at every meal, it is cheap and fills you up, but does not contain all the nutrients that a body needs to be healthy, so many people get sick because of poor diet.

Saturday

Today I have woken up waiting in anticipation to see what God is going to go today. After breakfast and prayer, I am now sitting waiting to be picked up on African time! Yesterday the pick-up time was 9 am, then this morning it changed to 11 am and as I am writing it is now nearly midday and still no pastor in sight! For new visitors to Africa, these things can seem frustrating and strange, as in the west, we are used to keeping time and if we are told 9am, we are ready by 9 am but not in Africa. I have to admit that even after all these years of working in Africa, I still find these things difficult although I am used to them by now, but it makes it difficult to know what time you should be ready by. If you delay thinking that the lift will be late then they might surprise you and come on time but most of the time, you get ready and find yourself sitting around waiting for hours which can be very frustrating but most of the time, the ministry that you experience when you get there, makes up for the frustration of what I now call "African time"!

Our lift has now arrived – Day 2 begins.

Saturday conference in Chitipa

In the afternoon I spoke about divine turn around and breaking the spirit of delay and many people responded to receive prayer.

During the lunch break, 2 pastors who had come about 100km to attend the conference began to share how I had prophesied over them in 2017 and that the things I had said came true. One pastor shared that I had prophesied about him starting a ministry and at the time he was just in a youth ministry but since that time, he began the ministry, and it has continued to grow up till this day. It is always encouraging when you hear that things you said or did many years ago are still bearing fruit in people's lives.

Before we began the evening session, we handed out a bag full of children's clothes that we had brought from the UK. It was wonderful to see some of the children receiving items of clothes and shoes and the delight that a small gift that would be insignificant in the UK could bring to a child in Africa. Many children walk around without having any shoes at all, so even just a basic pair of second-hand shoes is a big blessing to them. I always try to use up my baggage allowance to bring extra things to hand out and invariably usually end up at the oversize department at Heathrow due to the size of my bags. I usually try to bring the gifts in a laundry bag and then have it wrapped at the airport as there is no weight to the bag so you get your whole allowance of weight and can bring more things. So being able to witness the children receiving what we had brought was wonderful.

Then in the evening session there were 60 people who responded for salvation and many others were healed. One lady had been in a car accident in 2019 and had been left with leg pains but now all the pain had left her body. Several others testified that they were experiencing pain from their hips going down their legs but after prayer, the pain left, and they began to run in the church.

Then I felt that God wanted to heal ears, so I called people with ear problems to come forward and several responded. One lady testified that she had experienced blocked ears since childhood but after prayer, her ears opened and now she could hear properly. Another lady had one blocked ear but after prayer, she said that she felt like something moving out of her ear and now she could hear properly. Another lady said that she had been experiencing sharp pains in her ears but now all the pain had gone.

Then there was a lady who could not see properly, and I had to pray several times for her just like when Jesus prayed for someone who was blind and they said, "I see people looking like trees". When people tell me that they feel a bit better or pain is reducing, I often pray again until a complete healing comes because I believe that what God has begun, he will complete. So, I prayed again for this lady and after some time, she said that she could now see clearly and began to describe and read things that were in the distance.

Sunday morning in Chitipa

Sunday mornings in Chitipa are always a glorious time as the church is nearly always standing room only and the church is busy building an extension on the church to accommodate everyone that wants to come to church. This morning I preached on the return of the Lord and over 70 people came forward to receive Jesus. Then I began to pray for the sick.

There was a lady who had her leg in a cast and was walking with crutches as she had fallen 18 feet into a pit and injured her leg. I instructed her to sit on a chair and I began to pray for her leg. As I put my hands on her leg and prayed, her leg began to shake violently. Then she told me that the pain was reducing so I continued to pray. Then she said that all the pain had left, and she was able to get up without the crutches and join the worship team dancing! I then told her that she should go back to the hospital to ask them to remove the cast so that she could see that she was healed.

At the end there was much joy as she came to give her testimony and the crutches were held up in the air as a witness to what God had done.

Two weeks later a further testimony came through from the pastor in Chitipa – that same lady went back to the hospital as I had instructed her, and she had the cast removed. She then came back to church to testify that she is now completely healed. Every testimony is wonderful, but there are some that make you want to do a little dance around the room which I did. God is so amazing, and he still does miracles if we can believe.

The conference ended with much rejoicing as everyone came forward to bring gifts to us and to show their appreciation. Often the gifts involve the giving of African cloths which they delight in wrapping around us as everyone is dancing. A wonderful end to a wonderful conference.

Women's Refuge

On Monday we went to visit the women's refuge and see how the ladies are getting on and to also take some toiletry bags that someone in the UK had given me to bring for the ladies which included soap, flannel, toothbrush and toothpaste and some deodorant. All the bags were gratefully received. We were also able to assist one lady who had had all the items for her bakery business stolen in a burglary and she was very grateful to be able to have the ability to purchase what she needed to start her small business again making doughnuts to sell in the marketplace. After encouraging them, we walked around the land and prayed asking God to release the funds needed to be able to expand the work that is taking place. Even on this day, another older lady who had been widowed and had nowhere to go, came asking if there was a place for her at the house.

We have also recently been able to assist the women with bags of maize seed to plant in their small gardens that they have, and this is such a big blessing which has come just at the right time as it is planting season now just before the rainy season begins. Recently the women also learnt how to make their own compost so receiving these seeds will be a big blessing to them and will help them to not only have food to eat in the coming year but hopefully they will have a crop large enough that they can also sell some to make a living as well.

Branch church visit

On Monday afternoon we travelled out of Chitipa to a village about half an hour away called "Gideon". This was the place where a few years ago I gave one older lady some money to buy 2 chickens. Since that day the lady is now having many chickens and having eggs to eat and to sell as well as selling some of the chickens as they produce. Even this time, that same lady testified that those chickens are still sustaining her life. It is amazing in villages; how small things can help people.

Laurie who was travelling with me on this trip, taught the children about how God wants to be really close to us and be our friend. All the children were captivated by what he had to say and at the end, he went and sat in the middle of them to show them how God wants to come close to them. This had a big impact on not only the children but on the whole church who commented that he had taught the church about humility.

Travelling to Mzuzu

On Tuesday it was time to say bye bye to Chitipa and travel south to Mzuzu. Along the way we passed through many bumpy roads including a section where there is a mountain pass that goes high above Lake Malawi with stunning views. Before entering the mountain pass, we stopped at a local roadside market to buy bunches of bananas to feed the monkeys along the way. It is always fascinating to see the way the monkeys run along the side of the car, waiting for us to throw bananas out of the window.

As we were in this section of the mountain, the driver began to notice that the car was making some funny noises! Not a good place to break down! Sometimes you see trucks stuck there for 2 days before help comes. So, we made it to a safer place to stop while the driver got out to see what the problem was. A group of local young men also came over to see what was happening and began to assist us looking at the car. After about an hour of several men banging different things with spanner's, we decided to start off again and amazingly the funny noise seem to have reduced significantly. By the grace of God, we managed to reach Mzuzu by the end of the afternoon and check in to our hotel. Going to Chitipa is something that requires a good 4/4 in order to travel safely, and this has been our prayer for a long time. May God give us the tools for the job. Another prayer of mine has been that the redundant airports that are now closed in the northern region, will open again. To go to Chitipa by plane instead of road, would make such an amazing difference to our ministry here. A journey that takes 2 days, could be done in one hour.

When we were in Chitipa, we prayed over a runway that is now obsolete and prayed for it to become an operational runway again in Jesus' name.

Maybe God will even give us our own small plane as well as a 4/4. God owns everything and there is nothing impossible when we are committed to doing his work.

14. Ministry in Mzuzu and Mzimba

So, after resting on Tuesday, Laurie departs for Lilongwe on Wednesday morning to catch his flight back to the UK on Thursday and I continue with ministry in Mzuzu.

In the afternoon, we visited a small fellowship that I have been to many times in Mzuzu, and I enjoy going there as the people are very hungry to hear the word of God and come with their bibles and notebooks which is unusual in a lot of the places that I go to in Africa. So, because I knew their hunger to learn, I gave a more in-depth teaching on the end times and the return of the Lord.

Before I began teaching, I asked if anyone had a testimony from when I was there last year and one lady testified that last year she was suffering with ulcers, but after I prayed for her last year, now she can eat anything that she wants without having any pain. It is wonderful when you hear testimonies that have lasted like that.

After the word, many responded to receive anointing and prayer for other needs in their life and there was one man who had been a Muslim but that day, he decided to give his life to Jesus. He had been experiencing a lot of problems in his marriage and was crying out to God to help him. My heart went out to him, as he lay crying on the floor after receiving prayer. May God hear the cry of that young man's life. Afterwards the pastor of the church presented him with a bible, and I pray that he will move forward in his new life and that God will reveal the plans that he has for his life.

Ekwendeni

On Thursday and Friday, we travelled about 30 minutes from Mzuzu to a place called Ekwendeni. This is a place where I helped to establish a branch church several years ago. At the time, the church mostly consisted of the pastor and his family, so we went there to do an open-air meeting in the market place and several people responded to the message of salvation and from that time the church has been growing and moving forward, so it is always interesting to visit and see how they are getting on. Since my last visit, they have now moved from a temporary structure next to the pastors' house to a land that they have now bought and where they want to not only construct a church, but they are also planning to build a school which can not only serve the community but also bring in an income for the church through the school fees. The pastor has a great vision and up until now, he has mostly funded it himself through his business running a shoe shop in town. So, at lunch time we went to visit his shoe shop and obviously had to buy some shoes to support his business. Any excuse for shopping!

During the meetings here, several people testified to healing including the local chief who was healed of heart problems and was so overjoyed to be healed that he kept shaking my hand and thanking me for coming. Another man was healed of chest pains and another lady testified that she always had sleepless nights but after prayer the previous day, now she slept peacefully all night.

I noticed that in these meetings that over half of the congregation was children, so I also decided to have a special time to speak to the children before speaking my main message. On the first day I spoke about how Jesus comes looking for the one lost sheep and how he cares for us so much that when we are sad, lonely and hurting, he comes looking for us. On the second day, I spoke about the parable of the Good Samaritan and how God wants us to be kind and help people. All the children sat attentively listening to me and I am sure that God was touching their hearts through these stories. I always find that in Africa, it is far easier to talk and get the attention of children than it is in the West where children have so many other things to take their attention but here, they are interested to hear. It maybe also helps that I am white as that always seems to be a big attraction for children here especially in the villages. Often when we enter a village, the children will begin running and shouting "Mzungu, Mzungu", which means white person. In the past, it used to intimidate me, but I later learnt that it is a cry of excitement as they feel excited thinking that you have come to help them. This belief goes back to when the first white missionaries came to Africa, and they built schools and hospitals and brought the gospel. Indeed,Malawi was ruled by the British in the past so there is still a mindset in many that when white people come, they have come to help. This can have its advantages and disadvantages. The advantage can be that they listen and easily accept what you have to say, but the disadvantage can be that they often assume that you have a lot of money which of course is not usually the case so this is a mindset from the past that needs to be broken.

Saturday

On Saturday we had a conference in Mzuzu at a lady bishops church where we have been several times before and we had an amazing day of salvation, healing and deliverance.

As I woke up that morning, I asked the Lord what he wanted me to speak about that day and all I heard was the word "feet"! So, I began praying and was wondering what this could mean but as I meditated upon the word, suddenly I got a revelation of what God wanted me to share. I saw that feet in the bible are very significant and that God speaks a lot about feet. Feet carry authority, God said he would give us every place we set our feet. Feet bring proclamation, how beautiful are the feet that bring good news. Feet are anointed. Feet carry position, we have been raised up with Christ and all things are under our feet.

As I went with this revelation, I began the morning session by talking about Mephibosheth who was crippled in both feet because his nurse had dropped him when he was 5 years old and how many people are crippled emotionally because someone has let them down throughout their lives. Many people related to the message and much healing and deliverance took place in the morning session as God was setting people free from pain of the past and giving them a revelation that he has called us out of Lo Debar to sit at the Kings table with everything restored to us and lifted us up to a place of honour.

20 people gave their lives to the Lord and several people were healed including a lady who had swelling and pain in her side for 2 years but after prayer all the swelling and the pain went. Another lady testified to healing from back pains.

In the afternoon I spoke about how beautiful are the feet that bring good news and how God wants to anoint our feet to take the gospel of good news. Then I anointed everyone's feet, and many said that they felt God touching them as they were anointed. God directed me to use water and to have everyone line up and put their feet in a bowl while I poured water on their feet. It was a wonderful end to a wonderful day.

Feet washing is a very biblical concept that Jesus himself taught us to do.

Sunday at El Shaddai Temple

On Sunday we went to minister at a church in town where I went several years ago, and we had a glorious time with God doing many miracles. I will seek to highlight a few of the things that the Lord did on this day.

As we entered, I saw that they were in the process of building which is very common in Africa and there were bricks piled up at the back and at the front of the church. As you travel around Africa, you often see half-built buildings where people have begun to build and then they have run out of money, so the building just gets left, or people are just building slowly as finances allow them to. With houses and indeed churches, the people begin using the buildings even before they are finished which we would never do back home but here it is just a common thing. As soon as a building has a roof and a door, they just move in and then keep on building as they are able to.

Then I noticed that half of the congregation were children as again is often the case in Africa. African families often have many children and although this is a blessing, it can also be a burden as children in Africa cost a lot of money as they have to pay school fees which becomes one of the biggest bills for African families causing a lot of stress for a lot of people. You often hear parents talking about how they are looking for ways to pay school fees. Africa also has a culture of extended family as well, where uncles, aunts, sisters, brothers etc often become responsible for other relatives if one is struggling or has died.

Again, it can be a blessing that there is a support network within families, but it can also become a huge strain on the one who is doing well.

The children came forward to perform a few songs and then went to sit back down and most churches don't seem to have a Sunday school where the children actually go out to their own service but usually stay within the main service. This is probably because there is no other building to take them to. In some places I have noticed that they just take them to sit under a tree but in most places, the children just sit in the main service. So, I decided to call the children forward and speak a story to them from the bible before commencing my main message where I spoke on God doing impossible things.

I then began to call people forward for healing and then God gave me a word about a lady with pain down the side of her face and how God wanted to heal her. A lady then came forward crying and saying that she had pain down her face that started inside her mouth and even went down the side of her body. My initial reaction was that it was an abscess from her teeth, but she said that she had been to a dentist and been told that her teeth were ok. She also went to the hospital, but they didn't seem to know what was wrong. As I prayed for her, she said that she felt the pain leaving her body, so I continued to pray until all the pain had left her body, and she was free from pain. Afterwards she came to give her testimony and I was amazed at what she said. She said that the pain had started some time back and she had been to different hospitals to try to find a solution but to no avail. Then she decided to pray and fast about the situation and God told her that she would be healed. Then a few days before the meeting, she said that she had a dream and, in the dream, God told her "I am sending a minister to you and that minister will pray for you and you will be healed" Wow! I was so touched that God had shown her that I was coming, and Sunday was her day of deliverance. Hallelujah!

I remember one time several years ago, when someone said something similar but, on that occasion, they said that they actually saw me in a dream before I came. God is so amazing how he does things.

Then there was a lady who had swelling in her stomach for 2 years and every time she tried to eat something, her stomach would swell and be painful. As I began to pray for her, she acted like she was going to be sick, but afterwards she said that all the pain and swelling had gone.

Then there was a lady who said that she had a burning sensation in her feet, but after prayer, all the pain went. Before praying I had also asked her if she had received Jesus and she said "No", so I asked her if she would like to and she said "yes", so after first receiving Jesus, then she was also healed.

After noticing that several people in the line for healing, were also receiving Jesus, I then decided to give a call for salvation (something that I normally do in most meetings) but on this occasion the time had not seemed right after the preaching, but God's time was after I began praying for people. So, as I gave the call for salvation, 14 people came forward to receive Jesus.

I came back from the service knowing that God had truly changed people's lives that day.

On Monday, we went to sort out some land issues and then took the rest of the day to rest which was wonderful after the last few weeks of travelling and ministering.

On Tuesday we went to a small fellowship that met next to the Pastors house. I have noticed that if the church is new or they don't have enough money to either rent somewhere or build, then sometimes they just put up a small shelter next to their house in what we would call their yard and they set up church complete with P.A system so the whole neighbourhood can hear what is taking place. Of course, that would not be allowed in the UK, and you would soon have the neighbours complaining that you are making too much noise especially on a Sunday where most people in the west are resting but here In Africa, church and noise is seen as normal. I would not want to live next to it all the time as I do like peaceful environments but from the point of view of mission, it has its advantages. As you are preaching the gospel, you are aware that you are not just speaking to the people in front of you but probably all the houses nearby can also hear you as well. I noticed several people coming at the back to look around the corner to see what is happening. The fact that I am white, often causes a fascination as well especially with children. Some young children have never seen a white person before and most of the time they are fascinated but sometimes I have seen children look at me and run away screaming because they are frightened. Maybe they think they have seen a ghost!

As I began to preach, I saw the hunger of the people as they began responding and I knew that God was going to do miracles. As I gave the call for salvation, 6 ladies responded to receive Jesus and I then began praying for the sick. I had a word of knowledge that God wanted to heal knees. 2 ladies came forward and received healing and others were also healed of back pains and neck pains.

Then some of the leaders came forward for prayer including one of the pastors and I began to prophesy that he would be involved in oil business. Later he testified that he is a consultant and is in discussions with oil companies in the UK about bringing their business to Malawi. I was amazed that not only what I had seen was true, but the connection to the UK was even more amazing. His discussions were with a company in the UK, and I came prophesying about it from the UK. How amazing is that! So, we watch this space to see what God will do in that man's life.

Then I noticed that 2 young ladies had come late and were standing at the back of the church, so I asked them if they had come for prayer. They said that yes, they had come for prayer, so I invited them to come forward and asked them what they wanted prayer for, and they said that they wanted a prophecy and also favour in their lives. I can't remember everything I said but when I prayed for one of the ladies, I kept seeing the number 10, so I asked her about 10 and she said, "we are 10 children in our family"! I don't know exactly why God wanted to say that, but I felt that maybe it was just so that she would know that God knew everything about her and was with her. Sometimes, things that seem insignificant to us, can actually be a great encouragement to others. I want to encourage those of you who are involved with praying for others that sometimes we get a word that seems small or not relevant and we fail to share it. Like just seeing the No 10 and nothing to go with it, I nearly didn't say anything because I couldn't work out what God was trying to say, but as we share what we have by faith, it can be a big blessing to someone else. Also, don't try to add what God has not said. In my mind I was trying to think about

10 plagues, 10 commandments but God did not want me to add or make up what I thought 10 meant but to simply say what I saw and as I did, the young lady was very touched and put her own interpretation upon it as immediately she connected that they were 10 children in her family and God was speaking to her through that and showing her that he knew her and her family intimately. Sometimes, one word is all that someone needs – just give what God gives you to give and leave the rest up to him.

So, I came back from that meeting very encouraged with how God had spoken into people's lives. The gift of prophecy has the power to change people's lives and bring encouragement when it is done properly. The bible says that we should earnestly seek the gifts and especially those that build up the body of Christ. The gifts are not for ourselves but to edify the body of Christ, therefore let's ask God to give us gifts that we can use for the glory of his Kingdom and to bless others.

Mzimba

On Wednesday we travelled to Mzimba and began a series of meetings there. On our arrival, we went straight to a meeting that was already in progress and they were just waiting for us. They had planned to have an open-air outreach meeting but unfortunately, we had thunderstorms and rain, so it had to be cancelled and we met in a small building next to the pastor's house. In the morning I spoke on God of miracles and several people responded for salvation and then I began to pray for the sick and one lady testified that she had a swelling like a lump in her stomach that was very painful but after prayer the pain had gone.

On the way back for lunch, it was raining heavily, and the roads had started to become impassable in places, and we saw a car struggling to get up a muddy hill and eventually giving up and sliding back down the hill. There was a truck carrying several people out in the open in front of us and we watched as it tried to go down and then skidded on some rocks and swerved and nearly turned over but somehow managed to stay upright and continue on its journey. We managed to get down safely but decided that we would not attempt to take that route on the way back after lunch and luckily there was another route that we could take to avoid driving on hills. This is a huge problem in Malawi and indeed a lot of Africa, when the rains come on some roads, they become impossible to pass as a lot of village and rural roads are not tarmac so they easily become muddy and slippery causing a lot of problems to navigate and can also cause a lot of damage to the cars. So many cars don't last long here due to the bad road conditions and certainly some of the roads here, I would never attempt to drive my car on them, so this can be a huge challenge here.

In the afternoon, I spoke on Lazarus coming out of the grave and having his grave clothes removed. I find that this story often speaks to a lot of people as many people have received Jesus but have not been fully set free from their past which represents the grave clothes. I always find it interesting that Jesus did not take off Lazarus' grave clothes but told the people standing near to take them off and let him go. God has given authority to the church to set people free and to release healing in their lives. Jesus gave power and authority to his disciples and told them to preach the good news of the Kingdom and to heal the sick and cast out demons. Notice, he didn't tell the disciples to pray for the sick, he told them to heal them. The difference is that we are not asking God to do something, but we are taking the authority that he has given us in his name.

After the message a lot of people responded for prayer to be set free from their past and also to be set free from generational curses which is very prevalent in Africa due to a lot of idol worship that takes place.

It was still raining heavily as we left but we managed to make it back safely to our hotel by using a different route that did not involve driving up or down hills!

Thursday – Day of Another Lesson In African time

On Thursday we travelled to a village church near Mzimba, and this was a day of frustration and another lesson in how to have patience with ministry in Africa. We travelled in the morning and arrived at 10.30 expecting a morning service to already be underway but when we arrived, we found that the church was locked and only the assistant pastor and his wife were there, but they didn't have a key. Another frustrating thing that I often find is lack of communication. It seems that they were obviously not expecting us until the afternoon, but no one had communicated maybe because of network problems in the village but also in villages, there is not much concept of time compared with in town. In villages, most people are farmers, so morning is when the sun comes up and evening is when the sun goes down. Most probably don't own a watch and it is only maybe because most people have mobile phones now that they even look at the time at all. Church services do not start at any set time, they start when people appear and begin singing and slowly people begin to hear the music and are drawn to the church by the sound of the music and singing. So, after some time someone arrives with a key, and I assume that we will now start but we continue to wait without being told exactly what is happening. This is another frustration that I find. Sometimes people don't give details of what is happening, and you are just left wondering what is going on. We waited until 2 pm before they eventually decided that we should start. There were only a handful of people which is unusual so maybe they were delaying hoping that more people would come, but I said that I would rather speak to whoever is there rather than waiting all day not knowing if people are coming or not. Also, by this time I could see that dark clouds were gathering, and it was going to rain soon. As we were in a village, I was concerned about the car getting stuck if it rained heavily so I was eager to just begin something before it rained. As I began speaking, the winds began blowing strongly and I knew it was about to rain.

We are now in planting season and the beginning of rains so probably many people had decided to go to their fields to plant their maize seeds which could have contributed to the low number in church that day.

In the morning before I went, I was praying and felt God say that there would be someone with pain in the side of their mouth, so before I began my word, I spoke this word of knowledge and 2 people responded. One man said that he had been having pain in his teeth causing pain on the side of his face for over a year but as I prayed, all the pain went. Then another lady said that she had been having teeth pain for a while but again as I prayed, all the pain went. Jesus spoke about leaving the 99 sheep to look for the 1 and I knew that all the delays and hanging around had been worth it to bring healing to those people who had been in pain.

Then I spoke about having a dream for your life and I asked the people how many of them had a dream for their life and only 1 person put up their hand which I thought was very sad that most had no idea of aspiring to anything other than their day-to-day routine. I shared from the book of Genesis concerning Joseph and how he had a dream at 17 years old, but God had to take him through the process before he was ready to receive the fulfilment of the dream. Nearly everyone came forward to receive prayer for God to give them a dream for their lives. In a country that lives mostly below the poverty line, most don't have the luxury of dreaming, they are happy if they just make it through another day of surviving. In towns, many more are exposed to things that are going on in the world and are more likely to have ambitions but in villages, most don't have any other ideas of life apart from what they have always known. There are some things that are good, and it is a simple life away from a lot of cares that we often worry about in the west. I always feel a peace in the villages and certainly the people are very hospitable and will give you what they have.

According to their culture and hospitality they now wanted to serve us with a meal before we left but by this time, it was raining heavily, and I asked if we could please depart so that we would not have a problem on the road. The people were trying to persuade us to stay and saying that there would be no problem on the road (a story I have heard many times, and it is not true!). I knew that under normal circumstances, it was very rude to refuse to stay for a meal especially as I knew that they had slaughtered chickens specially for our meal which is a great honour. Most people in villages, only eat meat on special occasions or when an honoured guest arrives and under normal circumstances I would never refuse to stay and eat a meal that had been prepared but neither did I fancy being stuck somewhere on the road in a thunderstorm when it would be getting dark. So, after some discussions, we got in the car and departed back to our hotel arriving safely in time for dinner at the hotel.

Friday

On Friday we travelled to Kasungu where we stayed overnight so we could be nearer to where our Saturday conference would be. We had another lesson in patience as after checking in to the hotel, we went to the restaurant to have lunch and although there was a menu with a few things on it (never get excited about menu's when you are out of town)! So, we ask them what foods they have available, only to be told that they don't have any food available at the moment. For myself I did not mind too much as I had a big breakfast earlier but for the bishop and the driver, they were hungry. Eventually, they said that they could make some chicken if we waited 30 minutes which turned out to be more like an hour. They apologised and said that in the evening they were having a bbq and everything would be available. So, I got excited thinking that it will be a bbq like in the UK! So, around 6 pm, we head in the direction of the bbq and can't see much activity. Eventually a man appears and shows us 2 pieces of chicken! And accompaniments must be ordered separately at the restaurant. After several weeks in the villages, I was beginning to feel like a good steak! But we ate the chicken with chips as it was all that was available. I also keep reminding myself that we are very privileged and that many people here don't get to eat any meat, only on special occasions if they are lucky.

The next morning after breakfast, which was egg and chips again, we proceed to a place called Malembo where we were having a day conference. I spoke on "Is anything too hard for the Lord?" and a lot of people responded for salvation. Then I began to pray for the sick and God began doing miracles.

There was a lady with burning pain in her feet, but after prayer, she began to walk around the church without any pain.

Another lady was not able to read clearly and had to hold the book away from her when reading, but after prayer she was able to hold the book close to her and read clearly.

There were others that received deliverance from demons and many others that testified to various pains leaving their bodies after prayer.

In the afternoon, I spoke on God turning our unbelief laughter into a rejoicing laughter from the story of Abraham and Sarah who had a child in their old age. Many responded for prayer for God to breakthrough and turn situations around in their lives.

I had a word for a lady who was sitting at the back about restoration but when I called her forward, I noticed that she was wearing a black T Shirt with the words "school of witchcraft and wizardry" on it, so I asked her if she knew Jesus and she said that she did. So, then I asked her why she was wearing such a T Shirt, and she said that she did not realise what it said. I explained what it was and told her, that she needed to burn it and not wear such things as they will invite bad things into her life and keep the blessing of God away. I believe that God will begin working in that lady's life after this revelation was given to her. It is interesting that she was sitting right at the back, so I couldn't see her T shirt until she came forward, but God saw her and her situation and knew what needed to change. God sees us even from afar and he knows everything about our lives.

After the service, we then continued to drive back to Lilongwe where I would complete the last week of my mission.

15. Ministry in Lilongwe

On Sunday we visited a church and God began to do amazing miracles again.

There was a real atmosphere of the presence of God, and I knew that angels had walked into the room to do creative miracles. I had a word about lungs and the bishop's wife responded that she had suffered with asthma most of her life. After praying, she said that she felt she could breathe better, so by faith, I am believing that God has touched her life.

Then there was an older lady who had fallen and broken her arm and it had not healed properly, but after prayer, she began to move her arm without pain and then proceeded to pick up a bag and hold it in her hand which she couldn't do before.

Then I had a word about someone with a painful hand and a lady responded and was healed. Then I had words about pain at the bottom of the stomach after an operation, a word about a heart not beating properly and both of them responded and were healed. Another lady with pain in her legs began to lift them up and down without pain and a young boy who had damaged his foot, now began to run in the church without pain. Nearly every person that received prayer, testified that they had received healing.

The last few trips, I have definitely seen an increase in instant healings taking place and I pray that it will continue more and more as God demonstrates his kingdom, not only in words, but with signs following as well. As we are in the end times, I believe that more and more people will be brought into the Kingdom of God and that we will see the glory of God being seen around the world. God says in Isaiah 60 v 1 which is the scripture for this ministry of World Arise – "Arise, shine for your light has come and the glory of the Lord rises upon you". When darkness covers the earth, the glory of God will also increase. When it is dark, people look for the light. I believe that in the darkness that we see increasing, many will begin to search for the light. As children of God, we carry that light and as we go, many will be brought into the Kingdom of God.

Monday

Monday is usually a resting day, so I swam and enjoyed all the things that I had missed while I was out of town. I enjoy swimming and especially in a hot country, it is the best form of exercise. However, you mostly find swimming pools in town, so this is something I miss when travelling. Some hotels out of town, do have pools but they are often small and also dirty and not well maintained. I think because swimming is not really an African sport, so most places out of town don't bother with swimming pools. So, when I am back in town, I do enjoy swimming.

Then in the afternoon, I went with a friend for lunch at a local hotel.

Tuesday

On Tuesday we had a meeting at a church in one of the areas of Lilongwe and I spoke about how God takes care of his people even in the midst of a famine. With the recent devaluation, I have been trying to encourage people that if they trust God, he will take care of them.

On this evening, we had a problem with the electricity and halfway through preaching, all the lights and power went out leaving me preaching in the dark and without any microphone, which can often happen in Africa, so I just carried on while people were trying to find torches on their phones. Despite the issue with the lights, people still responded to receive Jesus and then people began getting healed as well.

One lady had pain in her ankle and knee and as I prayed, all the pain went. Then a lady who had pain around her back and waist, but after prayer, all the pain also went. Another lady had pain in her stomach from gas build up, but she had a powerful encounter with God, and I believe that she is healed.

This church is in an area of very bad roads and as we were leaving, we nearly got stuck in big ridges just trying to get out of the car park of the church. I often wonder why God takes me to such places, but it seems to also be the places where I see the most miracles. I guess that Jesus also went to the unreached areas and the places where people were forgotten and that's where people received him.

Right now, the roads in Lilongwe are very bad because they are doing construction of new roads but at the moment most of the roads have been dug up but not much progress being made (another Africa slowness!) which is making driving around Lilongwe very difficult and as they are now entering rainy season, it will become a nightmare as the dust will turn to mud where the roads have been dug but not completed.

However, we arrived back safely and now looking forward to what God is going to do next.

Wednesday

Today I decided to treat myself to some of the things that I had missed while I was travelling out of town, so took myself to the Wimpy bar and had a burger and fries followed by a yummy peanut butter sundae ice cream which was delicious. I am not someone who usually eats this kind of food as I try to eat healthy foods most of the time but sometimes when the choice of food has been limited, these treats seem appealing! I remember when burger bars first started becoming available in the U.K that the Wimpy was the first to arrive and amazingly Malawi is one of the first countries that I have discovered doesn't have McDonalds which seem to be worldwide so Wimpy and also Steers are the burger restaurants in Malawi but only found in main towns.

In the evening, we returned again to the same church, and I had a word of knowledge about someone with damaged knees. A lady responded bringing her young son who had been hit by a car a few months back and had been left with pain in one of his knees. After prayer, he began to walk around the church without any problems, so we are believing that God has touched this child in a wonderful way.

On Thursday we also returned to this church and God released fresh anointing over the people and many received breakthrough in their situations, and this was my last meeting of the mission and so "Mission accomplished" and time to rest for a few days.

At the end of each mission, I try to reserve a couple of days of relaxation and reflection where I book myself into a nice hotel in town and swim and eat nice food and generally relax and take time to reflect over what God has done during the mission so I ended by relaxing for a couple of days at one of my favourite hotels in town before heading to the airport for my flight late Saturday night.

16. Reflections

Arriving back in the U.K which thankfully was not as cold as it could have been. I often find that arriving back during winter can be a shock to the system when you come from 30 degrees every day to zero or minus degrees. As you come off the flight, you can feel the cold hitting you, but thankfully on this occasion in December, it was a balmy 11 degrees in London! It has gone a lot colder since and now as I am writing this in January, it is minus degrees but at least my body has had time to get used to it and hopefully by next month I will be off again to warmer climates!

So here I am now in January taking time to reflect and pray over the coming year which God has shown me is going to be pivotal, so I am waiting in expectation to see what God is going to do.

My church here was happy to see me back and to hear all about the amazing things that God had been doing and it was good to spend Christmas with my U.K church and to also plan with them for the coming year as well as continuing the regular zoom meetings and also planning for conferences and itinerant ministry here in the U.K. as well as planning the next mission trips and planning the ongoing projects in the nations.

Helping Women out of Prostitution

As I came back, I was led to read an article in the newspaper about women in Malawi who had been forced into prostitution after the cyclone earlier this year. Many women had lost their husbands, their businesses, their houses and everything they had, so out of desperation, many resorted to prostitution just to survive and to feed their children. I read that this was happening predominantly in the south and the lakeshore areas where the cyclone had hit the worst although it is a problem across Malawi and indeed many countries around the world. Some of the women, sell fish but this involves them going to the lake shore where the fishermen come in, and some men take advantage of the women, by demanding sex in return for selling them the fish. As I was reading about this, my heart was touched and I knew that we needed to do something, even though I didn't know what we could do as we already have many commitments, and our finances are already stretched. As I continued reading, I felt that God was saying that even if we began by just helping a few, then God will help us to continue from that point. Sometimes, God just asks us to begin where we can and allow him to bring the increase. So, through one of the Pastors in the south, we identified 3 ladies who were in this situation. When the cyclone came, their husbands were killed, their houses were destroyed and they were left with nothing, so out of desperation they began to do prostitution just to survive. Upon hearing about my concern, the pastor called them to his office to find out their situation and how we could help. At present, we have managed to pay for 3 months rent on a house for them and given them some capital to begin a business selling grocery items at the market like tomatoes, onions, chickpeas etc.

They have also been attending church and are being discipled and counselled so we are hopeful that their lives will begin to change.

At present they are trying to slowly build up their new business although the profit that they are making is not enough to buy food which is highly inflated and to send their children to school, so we are still assisting them to top up their income so that they are not tempted to go back into prostitution. We are believing that as word goes out concerning these situations, that we will be able to help many more women like them.

God calls us to reach out to the needy, he hears the cries of the poor and the vulnerable. The bible commands us to look after widows and orphans in their distress and even if we feel that we can't meet all the needs in the world, we can begin by helping the one in front of us and then he will give us the ability to help two and then three. As we are faithful with small things, he will entrust us with many things.

As I plan to go back to Africa in a few weeks time, I am looking to see what God is going to do both spiritually and practically and praying that God will use us to reach many more people as we keep moving forward.

As I come to the end of this book, I am sitting on a cold but sunny day, soon heading for a 30 degrees sunshine and wondering what God is going to do next. In a few weeks I will be heading back to Uganda and Malawi, and it will be great to reconnect with all the wonderful people that I have been privileged to know over the years. I began by saying that everything is a step of faith, but I also know that every step that we take, God has already gone ahead of us and prepared the way. I hope that you have been inspired that God can use you to do great things and to change lives around the world.

Epilogue

I hope that you have enjoyed reading "Miracles in the nations". A book that God inspired me to begin writing last year to show you all the amazing things that God is doing around the world. It is my prayer that God has touched your heart as you have been reading.

My prayer is also that this may be just Part 1 of Miracles in the nations and that many subsequent books will come in the future as God expands the work that he is doing.

Mathew 28 v 19 "Therefore go and make disciples of all nations, baptising them in the name of the Father and of the Son and of the Holy Spirit "

Everything that I have written can be summed up in the above verse where Jesus gave the command to Go. I remember several years ago, a friend who used to come on mission trips with me but is now with the Lord, said these words. "What do Christians find so hard about the word GO"? Jesus did not tell us to pray for people to come, he asked us to go to them.

We cannot just sit in church and pray for the world, we must GO. Obviously not every person has the call or the ability to go around the world, but we can go to our local area, we can go to our friends and family, and we can support and pray for those who are going around the world.

The word Apostle literally means "sent one". I believe that in these end times, God is wanting to raise up an Apostolic army who will respond to the call of God to go to wherever he would send them and take the gospel to the dying and hurting people both spiritually and practically.

We see the example of Jesus and the example of the apostles, they did not just preach, but there was a demonstration of the Spirits power through the laying on of hands for healing and signs and wonders but also a demonstration of practical help. If you see your brother in need of clothes or food and you just tell him to go and keep warm, what good is that? We see that Jesus when he wanted to talk to 5,000, he also fed them as well as talking to them.

My prayer is that God will enable us to reach out to the lost and hurting with the good news of salvation and healing but also with practical ways of helping people.

My prayer is that you have been inspired to also make a difference wherever you are.

We cannot help everyone, but as the story of the boy with the star fish shows, we can make a difference to the one in front of us. I was walking along the beach near where I live a few months back and I saw this baby star fish on the sand. I decided to take a photo to use in this book because it reminded me that we can make a difference to the ones that God puts in front of us.

I was walking along the beach when I saw this and thought of the story - it made a difference to this one.

If you have been inspired and would like to help the ministry through prayer or support, you can get in touch through the email at the end of this book. If you would like prayer for a situation in your life, we would also like to pray for you and for details of my other books including -

Can I really know the Holy Spirit.
Healing
Knowing your identity
The Anointing
Restoring the Bride

Every one of us has a call upon our lives and as we step out in faith, God will reward us according to his word.

May the Lord bless you and show you the good plans that he has for your life.

For further details contact: -

Worldarise700@gmail.com

www.ingramcontent.com/pod-product-compliance
Lightning Source LLC
Chambersburg PA
CBHW052147110526
44591CB00012B/1885